'Steve Hall and Simon Winlow are quite simply the most important criminologists working in Britain today. The breadth of their vision, their scholarship and the certainty of their conclusions makes them both impossible to ignore and vital to understand. *Revitalizing Criminological Theory* is the latest in a growing list of extraordinary, insightful, passionate and beautifully crafted works that they have produced and I urge anyone who cares about criminology to read it.'

Professor David Wilson, Founding Director Centre for Applied Criminology, Birmingham City University, UK

'If you buy one criminology book this year make it *Revitalizing Criminological Theory* by Steve Hall and Simon Winlow. Criminological theory is at the crossroads, where bluesman Robert Johnson was supposed to have sold his soul to the devil. As the authors show in this book all previous criminology theory has sold its soul, including both neo-liberal and left liberal/postmodern criminology. If we are to move beyond this present dichotomy which has pervaded global criminology for decades, we need to follow the signpost out of this mess – it reads "ultra-realist criminology this way" and this text is its handbook.'

Professor Steve Redhead, Faculty of Arts, Charles Sturt University, Australia

'A vital and timely contribution on why a new criminology is needed. This slim and important volume casts new theoretical light on underlying causes of neoliberal-based harms of the powerful and abject. A much needed breath of fresh thinking.'

J. Robert Lilly, Regents Professor of Sociology, Northern Kentucky University, USA

REVITALIZING CRIMINOLOGICAL THEORY

This book provides a short, comprehensive and accessible introduction to ultra-realism: a unique and radical school of criminological thought that has been developed by the authors over a number of years. After first outlining existing schools of thought, their major intellectual flaws and their underlying politics in a condensed guide that will be invaluable to all undergraduate and postgraduate students, Hall and Winlow introduce a number of important new concepts to criminology and suggest a new philosophical foundation, theoretical framework and research programme. These developments will enhance the discipline's ability to explain human motivations, construct insightful representations of reality and answer the fundamental question of why some human beings risk inflicting harm on others to further their own interests or achieve various ends.

Combining new philosophical and psychosocial approaches with a clear understanding of the shape of contemporary global crime, this book presents an intellectual alternative to the currently dominant paradigms of conservatism, neoclassicism and left-liberalism. In using an advanced conception of 'harm', Hall and Winlow provide original explanations of criminal motivations and make the first steps towards a paradigm shift that will help criminology to illuminate the reality of our times.

This book is essential reading for academics and students engaged in the study of criminology, sociology, criminological theory, social theory, the philosophy of social sciences and the history of crime.

Steve Hall is Professor of Criminology at Teesside University and Co-Director of the Teesside Centre for Realist Criminology. In the 1970s he was a nomadic musician, general labourer and avid reader of anything political or philosophical. In the 1980s he worked with young offenders in the deindustrializing North-East of England, and he was politically active during the steelworks and mine closures in County Durham. In the 1990s he began teaching, researching and publishing. Essentially a criminologist, he has also published in the fields of sociology, history and radical philosophy. He is author of numerous articles and *Theorizing Crime and Deviance* (Sage, 2012), and co-author of *Violent Night* (Berg, 2006), *Criminal Identities and Consumer Culture* (Routledge, 2008), *Rethinking Social Exclusion* (Sage, 2013) and *Riots and Political Protest* (Routledge, 2015). He is co-editor of *New Directions in Criminology* (Routledge, 2012).

Simon Winlow is Professor of Criminology at Teesside University and Co-Director of the Teesside Centre for Realist Criminology. He completed his PhD at the University of Durham in the 1990s before commencing work as a researcher on the ESRC Violence Research Programme and a lecturer in criminology and sociology in various UK universities. He is the author of numerous articles and *Badfellas* (Berg, 2001), and co-author of *Bouncers* (Oxford University Press, 2003), *Violent Night* (Berg, 2006), *Criminal Identities and Consumer Culture* (Willan/ Routledge, 2008), *Rethinking Social Exclusion* (Sage, 2013) and *Riots and Political Protest* (Routledge, 2015). He is co-editor of *New Directions in Criminological Theory* (Routledge, 2012) and *New Directions in Crime and Deviancy* (Routledge, 2012).

NEW DIRECTIONS IN CRITICAL CRIMINOLOGY

Edited by Walter S. DeKeseredy, West Virginia University, USA

This series presents new cutting-edge critical criminological empirical, theoretical, and policy work on a broad range of social problems, including drug policy, rural crime and social control, policing and the media, ecocide, intersectionality, and the gendered nature of crime. It aims to highlight the most up-to-date authoritative essays written by new and established scholars in the field. Rather than offering a survey of the literature, each book takes a strong position on topics of major concern to those interested in seeking new ways of thinking critically about crime.

REVITALIZING CRIMINOLOGICAL THEORY

Towards a new ultra-realism

Steve Hall and Simon Winlow

LONDON AND NEW YORK

First published 2015
by Routledge
2 Park Square, Milton Park, Abingdon, Oxon, OX14 4RN

and by Routledge
711 Third Avenue, New York, NY 10017

Routledge is an imprint of the Taylor & Francis Group, an informa business

British Library Cataloguing in Publication Data
A catalogue record for this book is available from the British Library

Library of Congress Cataloging in Publication Data
Hall, Steve
Revitalizing criminological theory : towards a new ultra-realism / Steve Hall and Simon Winlow.
-- First Edition.
pages cm. -- (New directions in critical criminology ; 11)
1. Criminology. 2. Crime. I. Winlow, Simon. II. Title.
HV6018.H35 2015
364.01--dc23
2014040627

ISBN13: 978-0-415-74435-5 (hbk)
ISBN13: 978-0-415-74436-2 (pbk)
ISBN13: 978-1-315-81308-0 (ebk)

Typeset in Bembo
by Integra Software Services Pvt. Ltd, Pondicherry, India

If a way to the better there be, it lies in taking a full look at the worst
Thomas Hardy

CONTENTS

ILLUSTRATIONS

Figure

Tables

1

INTRODUCTION

This book's fundamental purpose is very straightforward. The intention is to persuade the reader that Western criminology needs to begin working towards a new theoretical framework which provides an enhanced explanatory capability fit for purpose in today's rapidly changing world. The era of the alleged 'international crime decline' might seem like an inappropriate time to suggest that criminology should revive its investigations of harm and criminal activities with renewed vigour. However, as we shall see in a little more detail later, this 'crime decline' is a misleading concept. It applies only to specific regions and nations, and remains trapped in the empirical realm of one-dimensional legally constructed definitions of crime that ignore a huge dark figure of ill-defined, systematically ignored, misperceived, non-criminalized, unreported and unrecorded harms. As the book's argument unfolds, we will suggest that if contemporary criminology intends to retain some sort of grip on a rapidly changing world, the concept of 'crime' is inadequate because in the neoliberal era the general zemiological field of harm is also changing rapidly, and many types of harm are becoming normalized, both in everyday life and the way they are represented by mass media and governments. These harms are opaque to the limited ethical and empirical apparatus that criminology currently uses to define, detect and explain what exists in the world.

The argument we put forward here is not simply the standard assault on the mainstream right-wing or centrist perspectives. What we now call 'critical criminology' grew out of a post-war canon of idealist left-liberal criminological theory – sometimes referred to as 'left idealism' (Young, 1975). In the 1970s, we will argue, because of over-investment in its sacred domain assumptions, which are rooted in hard-line social constructionism, this paradigm had already reached an intellectual impasse every bit as debilitating as that which ground conservative theory to a halt two decades earlier. We have challenged these assumptions in fine detail elsewhere (see Hall et al., 2008; Hall, 2012a; Winlow and Hall, 2013; Winlow et al., 2015), and interested readers are encouraged to follow up this book with explorations of these more complex works. However, the purpose of this book is to present an accessible stripped-down synopsis of these arguments and the foundations of a new theoretical framework that we have named *ultra-realism*. This framework can help criminology to produce more penetrative analyses of the world that neoliberalism – relatively unhindered by the least effective left-wing political opposition we have seen for over a century – is currently making for us.

We will not be suggesting that ultra-realism can open up a transparent, all-seeing God's eye view of the whole world, the totality in which we exist, or, indeed, even the whole world of crime and harm. Because inflicting harm on others is immoral and crime is illegal, and, obviously, being involved in either can provoke some sort of reprisal, perpetrators usually exert huge effort in concealing their actions. Thus the dark figure of unknown events is notoriously large compared to those associated with other major issues researched by social scientists. However, by cutting through the prohibitions placed on research and theorization by criminology's current dominant and subdominant authorities – i.e. neoclassical realism and left idealism – ultra-realism can open up *parallax views*, or new perspectives from previously obscured angles that create changes in the observational positions and displacements of the objects in view. Both the powerful and the abject social classes experience important concrete universal truths in their social spaces; truths that have been denied prominent positions in criminology's research programmes and storehouse of knowledge. It is the task of ultra-realist criminological research and theorization to open up these spaces and throw some light on revealed truths as symptoms of underlying causes and contexts.

In order to present the initial intellectual moves towards the ultra-realist position in a short, yet, we hope, comprehensive, adequately contextualized and accessible work suitable for students and researchers at all levels, we have constructed the chapters as follows. First, Chapter 2 will outline most of the mainstream classical and contemporary theories that can be found in the canon of criminological theory. Attention will be focused on the flaws that afflict these mainstream theories. However, our goal is not simply to dismiss all that has gone before and leave nothing in its place. Rather, it is to re-engage our disciplinary dialectic so that we can develop new ideas better suited to explaining crime and harm in our own unique conjuncture. To do this effectively we must return to informed critique that takes theory building seriously. It is now crucial that criminologists display the courage necessary to commit to informed intellectual positions and defend them honestly in a robust environment of productive critique that is capable of providing the forward motion our discipline so badly needs. We hope that our identification of the flaws of mainstream theories will pose an initial question in the reader's mind – if these mainstream theories are so flawed, why are many of them still used as frameworks for criminological analyses? This critique of mainstream criminological theories, aimed at their fundamental domain assumptions, should begin to make it clear to the reader why a paradigm shift to ultra-realism is necessary if criminological theory wants to offer more convincing explanations of its objects – crime and harm – and why they appear as they do in today's world.

Chapter 3 will outline the tradition of critical criminology. We will examine its growth as a broad spectrum of domain assumptions, theoretical approaches and research projects which revolve around the principle of structural imbalances in social power and analyses of the ways in which these imbalances are *ideologically constructed* in popular culture and the individual's mind – thus the 'idealist' core of the paradigm. The question we will pose here is whether critical criminology's current theoretical paradigm is up to the task of effectively opposing mainstream criminological theory and advancing the discipline forward. Given what we have said above, there is no prize for guessing that the answer is a qualified 'no', but the specific reasons *why* it can no longer fulfil these tasks must be laid out in basic detail before we can begin to move forward.

Of course this is not the first time that the inadequacies of left-idealist critical criminology have been exposed to critique. From the late 1970s onwards the paradigm of neoclassical realism, or right realism, dominated criminological thought in the so-called 'real world' of government, media and popular culture. A major reason for its success is that it received unwavering ideological support from the corporate right-wing press. However, another important reason is that many of critical criminology's claims, which revolved around the idealist notion that crime was merely a *social construct* ideologically concocted and hegemonically promoted by the right for its nefarious political purposes, seemed increasingly ludicrous to everyday people who were suffering the worst of the 'crime explosion' that occurred in Western nations in the 1980s as they deindustrialized. Chapter 4 will examine the various *radical realist* responses to left idealist and right realist criminological theories, which, beginning with feminist realism, victimology and left realism, expanded and gained some momentum and credibility in Western governmental circles in the 1980s and 1990s. The radical realist paradigm will be scrutinized in the same way as critical criminology – did it provide an effective political opposition to the right and centrist mainstream, as well as plausible contextualized explanations of contemporary forms of crime and harm?

Chapter 5 will examine the political and philosophical roots of both mainstream and critical paradigms in criminological theory, and how their flaws can be traced back to rigid domain assumptions rooted in traditional philosophical and political positions. Advocates of these positions have tried to impose upon us unshakeable ontological truths about human nature and the social world. Here we will also see how and why these paradigms are protected and reproduced in various institutional settings. This will provide a platform for chapters 6 and 7, which explain the *ultra-realist* position. By incorporating the new philosophical position of *transcendental materialism* and the new cultural-historical theory of *pseudo-pacification*, ultra-realism can advance the alternative paradigm of *critical realism*, hitherto seriously neglected and under-used in criminological theory, to a position where it can be adopted as a more revealing theoretical framework and research programme.

2

MAINSTREAM CLASSICAL AND CONTEMPORARY THEORIES

This chapter outlines the development of the main Western schools of criminological theory. The objective is to trawl through and outline their main principles, tensions and, most importantly, flaws in order to explain clearly why a shift through critical realist theory to ultra-realist theory is now essential.

Enlightenment thinking on law and crime was founded in the eighteenth century on the principle that all individuals are born with the God-given gifts of free will, universal reason and a moral sense, and it is each individual's personal responsibility and *duty* – expressed in Kant's (1998) famous deontological notion of the *categorical imperative* – to apply these gifts and obey a law that has been laid down by others who share them. Transgressors must be punished, in proportion to the serious-ness of the crimes they commit, for no other reason than they *deserve* punishment. This is all very well as a hopeful normative gesture, but it is of little use to criminological theory because it does not answer the fundamental question of *why* some people do not abide by the catego-rical imperative and the law. In Hume's (1967) parlance, the *ought* overwhelms the *is*: it tells us ideally what we *should do* but little about what we *actually do* in real life and why we do it, or, conversely, why we don't do it. Therefore from its beginnings Enlightenment criminological thought has been inherently and unshakeably *moralistic* and *idealist*.

These modern principles laid the philosophical foundation of the Western criminal justice system in the eighteenth century. However, their principal flaws are well-known (see Bean, 1981). First, certain important aspects of the law can be biased in favour of the powerful social classes, and can act against the relatively powerless, which suggests that the type of 'reason' that dominates in any given society is not universal but belongs specifically to the elite. The classical liberal-capitalist system, beholden to the notion of universal reason and individual morality, responsibility and choice as the sole causes of criminal acts, is blind to this social-structural tension. It is a system largely unreceptive to the social, economic and political contexts in which human action takes place. Second, the primacy of reason or conscious understanding in classical thinking either ignores unconscious drives and desires, or at least assumes that human beings are always in control of these powerful forces. The implications of this negligence are enormous – the basic principles and practices that govern the whole individualized, rationalized Western criminal justice system might well be based on faulty one-dimensional conceptions of human nature and the social structure (see Hall, 2012a). Basically, it is an avowedly idealist position with only a passing interest in contextual reality.

The philosophy of utilitarianism added a *naturalized* ontological, rationalist and consequentialist layer underneath classical liberal thinking, which in its Kantian variant was still governed by metaphysics, deontology and intrinsicalist morality – what this means in simple terms is that all individuals have a duty to conform to the law because it is the product of universal morality and reason and therefore an end in itself. Utilitarians were considerably less metaphysical, deontological and intrinsicalist. They were naturalistic, claiming that the human being is driven by natural instincts to avoid pain and seek pleasure. However, they also thought that human beings have the natural ability to rationalize and calculate the *consequences* of their actions, and the sensibilities required to distinguish between healthy and unhealthy forms of pleasure. The law must make sure that the *costs* of committing crime outweigh the *benefits*, which should deter the majority of individuals from committing crime and threatening the rights and property of others. This position is *consequentialist* because it moves beyond intrinsicalism to claim that both potential perpetrators and the onlookers of visible punishments base their actions on their predicted consequences. Therefore, on a broader social scale, the deterrent effect of the law can have consequences for individuals and their social lives. The law and its delivery of justice is not just an end in itself but can become a means to broader social – and, by extension, political – ends.

Utilitarianism, however, is contradictory at its ontological root. The claim that human beings are free-willed contradicts the basic premise that we are driven primarily by natural pleasure/pain instincts. In other words, we have choices but when we get down to the very fundamental choice over whether to put our own hedonistic interests first we do not. As we shall see later, this is an obsolete eighteenth century position that fails to understand how twentieth century consumer culture has manipulated and stimulated individuals' instinct for pleasure to the extent that it exerts pressure on the psyche, which shapes and intensifies desire and orientates it to external consumer objects. This inclines the individual to occasionally bypass the rational calculation of consequences and risk the high costs associated with illegal expressive and acquisitive activities (Hallsworth, 2006; Hall et al., 2008). In a nutshell, utilitarianism was an early form of naturalistic realism that tried to dig under metaphysical idealism to posit a real, natural basis for human nature but grossly over-simplified it and got it largely wrong. Therefore, as we shall see later, we need a far more sophisticated and realistic conception of human nature.

Classical liberalism did contain its own oppositional stance, founded on John Locke's notion of the individual as *tabula rasa*, a blank slate on which culture writes its scripts, which influenced the radical liberal position that we will encounter later. However, the first paradigm to develop in late nineteenth century Europe as a serious institutional challenge to the orthodox classical liberal notion of free will was *positivism* (Melossi, 2008). There were two main schools – bio-psychological and sociological positivism.

The field of bio-psychological positivism, developing from the mid-nineteenth century onwards, is a set of theories based on the principle that inherited predispositions to aggressive, impulsive and anti-social behaviour vary in intensity in different 'personality types' amongst individuals. These traits, which Lombroso (1876) argued are identifiable by outward physical manifestations or 'stigmata', are transmitted across the generations by genes. In the late nineteenth and early twentieth centuries, extreme right-wing and nationalistic political groups believed that these traits are identifiable in specific inferior cultural and social groups, which means that crime can be reduced only by eliminating these groups. Horrific political movements such as Nazism adopted this principle to gain pseudo-scientific credibility amongst their populations (see Rafter, 2009). This position ignores the *plasticity and adaptability* of the human neurological system, which, if true, demolishes biologism's foundational principle of heritable characteristics. We will investigate this in further detail later when we discuss *transcendental materialism*.

However, more enlightened biological theorists in the late nineteenth and early twentieth centuries, such as Enrico Ferri (1898), who was a left-wing socialist – and not, as Rafter (2009) claims, an unreconstructed follower of the biological determinist Lombroso – argued that the bio-logically innate impulses that lead to aggression and selfishness are latent aspects of everyone's basic constitution and can be triggered by specific environmental factors (see also Owen, 2012). Therefore Ferri argued that the causes of criminality can be found in the conditions in which some people live, not in unique inherited characteristics, and these conditions are the products of an unequal capitalist socioeconomic system. Of course, this cannot explain criminality amongst the powerful and well-to-do elite members of society, or different individual tendencies in the same conditions. Although contemporary forms of bio-psychological theorizing are more enlightened and less rigid (Meloni, 2014), in its traditional form it is one-dimensional and reductive, based on the sort of obsolete ontological conceptualizations of human nature from which new realist criminology must try to escape.

Sociological positivism is an early social scientific position that claims to be able to use scientific methods of observation, data production and data analysis to identify real causes and effects in the social world. From the mid-nineteenth century onwards it mounted one of the most serious challenges to classicism. Hard positivism claimed to identify direct causes for phenomenologically registered events. Soft positivism, a less deterministic doctrine, provided early social scientists with a set of *probabilistic* hypotheses and theories that identify less definite and less predictable but still analytically useful *tendencies* to commit crime or harm in certain social, cultural and economic contexts, which can be 'tested' by generating data to prove or disprove them. Durkheim (1970) famously suggested that suicide was more prevalent in Protestant societies, and therefore causes could be identified in Protestant culture and its reactions to social change. Bonger (1916) argued that crime and other social problems would tend to occur in impoverished environments that demoralized individuals at the same time as capitalism's mainstream culture created anti-social egotistical personality types. These tendencies vary according to differing social, cultural and economic conditions, such as differing religious or cultural values and norms, economic recessions, and communities disrupted by rapid economic change or the failure of social institutions such as families, schools and mass media to reproduce civilized values.

Durkheimian theory crossed the Atlantic to be developed in the 1920s and 1930s by early Chicago School sociologists, who focused on the notions of social disorganization and pathology. As immigrants moved into the chaotic and competitive 'zone of transition' in cities, their previously stable systems of morality and meaning were disrupted. The resulting 'moral dissensus' and anomie – a breakdown and fragmentation of meaning and moral guidance about what is right and wrong and an ensuing culture of 'normlessness' or disregard for society's norms and rules – combines with relative poverty to give rise to pathological behaviours including drug-taking, prostitution and crime. It's a probabilistic theory that both overstates its probability and therefore overpredicts crime, and narrows its focus far too much by suggesting that the 'zone of transition', with its transient and supposedly anomie-prone population, is the only social space in which anti-social values and meanings can become dominant. However, the reality is that despite the pressures of competition, relative poverty and instability, many people who live in this zone *do not* commit crime and others who live in relatively rich and stable parts of the city *do* commit crime. It's also a form of cultural reductionism that ignores the ability of politics to improve conditions in urban areas and of political institutions such as parties, unions and social movements to help create a culture of solidarity amongst individuals.

However, there is too much individual variation in criminality for direct, mechanistic causal links to be made between readily observable external conditions and criminal actions. The relationship between the individual and external conditions is always mediated by the complex systems of values, norms, rules and languages that make up culture. Bonger, often too hastily accused of being a determinist (Moxon, 2014), acknowledged this mediation in his work. As we shall see later, critical realists argue that at the deeper level causes are complex structures and processes that are not directly observable yet not simply cultural, therefore they require sophisticated conceptualization (Bhaskar, 1997). Positivists consistently fail to produce the sophisticated concepts needed to 'operationalize' their data and act as true indicators of observable social phenomena or their deep underlying causes. Therefore positivist data never really get underneath simplistic surface correlations, and lack sophistication and validity at the basic *conceptual* level, the foundation stone of social science.

The quantitative data that positivists produce about changes in crime rates are a classic example: they rely on narrow legally-defined conceptualizations of crime without asking whether they truly represent the harms that impact negatively on people's lives. Positivists rely on the recording of crimes by the police or the reporting of crimes by individuals selected to participate in victim surveys. They omit the broader non-criminalized harms inflicted on individuals and their social and physical environments every day, and they cannot possibly detect the full number of crimes or harms committed. The 'dark figure' of legally-defined crime that remains off the positivists' radar in Western nations is roughly estimated to be around 70 per cent (Coleman and Moynihan, 1996). Therefore their conceptualization of the phenomenon of harm is too narrow and partial, and their quantitative data have very little validity as representations of the totality of real events in the field of harm.

The claim that quantitative data are valid enough to test causal hypotheses is very dubious. Invalid quantitative data can be actively misleading, 'proving' hypotheses that are probably wrong and 'disproving' hypotheses that might be in some ways right. Because they lack validity yet appear to have high reliability (or 'generalizability') at regional, national or even international levels, quantitative data are extremely useful to politicians and their civil servants as means of ideological manipulation. Data can also be *presented* to the public by governments and the mass media in partial and very misleading ways; for instance, the media can trumpet an overall '7 per cent crime decline' without telling the population that crime statistics do not represent a lot of everyday crimes and harms, some of which might have actually increased in local residential areas that experience high crime rates above the national average.

However, in small doses soft positivism does have a limited use. If its knowledge claims remain modest, limited to correlations, strictly probabilistic and not causal, it can provide initial evidence that complex combinations of external conditions do correlate with significant changes in crime rates. For instance, in the neoliberal era in Britain and the USA from around 1980 the combination of deindustrialization, unemployment, fragmentation of communities and pressure placed on individuals by consumer culture correlated with a statistical 'crime explosion' that quite probably did indicate a significant increase in real events (Reiner, 2007; Hall and McLean, 2009; Currie, 2010). Positivism can never explain criminological phenomena, but it can flag up correlations that are worthy of further investigation using qualitative methods and sophisticated theory at a deeper level of conceptualization. On the back of these correlations complex multi-level *probabilities* that combine social, economic, cultural and psychological dimensions can be theorized (Hall and Wilson, 2014).

Strain theory, developing in the late 1930s through the 1940s and 1950s, attempted to include cultural mediation in an otherwise quasi-positivistic framework. Before pluralistic theories became dominant in the 1950s, it was possibly the most influential and enduring probabilistic criminological theory with vaguely 'critical' credentials insofar as it challenged mainstream classicism and positivism. The main architect, Robert Merton (1938), drew upon Durkheim's (1961; 1970) notion of 'anomie', a temporary condition of normlessness that occurs when rapid socioeconomic change disrupts systems of consensual values and norms and the institutional mechanisms that reproduce them, such as families, work and education. However, for Merton, anomie was a more enduring structural problem because the American Dream, a culture that promised material success for all US citizens if they worked hard, inflicted permanent strain on the individual's commitment to the sociable values and norms we need to live together as peaceful, law-abiding citizens. This strain was intensified during times when opportunities for individuals' socioeconomic advancement were blocked in an unequal social structure.

At the time this was an important intellectual move because it challenged the *integrationism* inherent in Durkheimian sociology and the US structural-functionalist sociology it spawned, a strange mixture of idealism and positivist causality which argued that any society can be a *harmonious whole* if institutions perform their primary task of reproducing consensual values and norms. Merton (1938) replaced this full-blown notion of integrationism with structural strain, which suggested that inequality caused disharmony, if not full-blown social conflict, in American society at the deep level of basic socioeconomic relations. As norms and values are disrupted and thrown into confusion, the cultural boundaries placed around human action are stretched and broken, allowing the natural tendency of the 'malady of infinite aspiration' to be activated to fuel anti-social egotism and various forms of deviant behaviour. Various subcultures splinter away from the norm as their opportunities to fulfil the American Dream and join the mainstream are blocked. Merton (1938) boiled these down to five main categories: conformity, ritualism, retreatism, innovation and rebellion. The final two are linked to crime: innovation because many forms of acquisitive crime require innovative business practices and rebellion because blocked opportunities can cause a reaction-formation that is anti-social and hostile.

However, despite its acknowledgement of structural socioeconomic disharmony and strain, strain theory still assumes a *consensual* rather than a *conflictual* or *plural* value system, and thus explains subcultures as splinters that break away from the norm as individuals encounter difficulties in their pursuit of similar goals. Therefore, for Merton (1938), only the means are plural while the ends are consensual, which makes the theory essentialist and universalist at its root and plural only on its surface. It is also a rationalist theory based on problem-solving, and therefore it can't explain vandalism, hate crime, violence or other irrational, visceral forms of crime. It has been said that the theory over-predicts criminality, but this is possibly a weak criticism because Merton (1938) was aware of alternative means of dealing with blockages. The common criticism that it cannot deal with crimes of the powerful is also weak. Moral systems can be disrupted and, because the malady of infinite aspiration is what it says – infinite – individuals can perceive blocked opportunities at any point in the social structure. Even at the very top they can imagine having more.

For us, the fundamental problems are twofold. First, Merton (1938) assumed that socio-structural inequality produces a blockage of opportunities fuelled by a *common interest* rather than a fundamental structural – not 'plural' – clash of interests based on capitalism's underlying logic and social relations between workers and capitalists. Up to the 1980s, we have argued, before the current era of *capitalist realism* – more about this later – many workers had a very different vision of society and therefore different interests (Hall et al., 2008). Second, although he recognized the American Dream as a cultural phenomenon, he followed Durkheim (1961) in assuming that the 'malady of infinite aspiration' and anti-social egotism are natural, innate and timeless human propensities, ready to pop out and shatter society's framework of norms whenever traditional cultural systems and economic opportunities are disrupted. We shall argue later that they are not natural in themselves but *psychosocially manufactured* and systematically brought to the fore only in combined socioeconomic and cultural systems that obstruct and repress the alternative human propensities for cooperation and solidarity by fostering anxiety and rule-bound types of hostile competitiveness. Merton (1938) saw politics as a means of increasing opportunities rather than creating solidarity and removing the pressure that the capitalist mass media and advertising industry exert on individuals in order to encourage them to compete against each other for status symbols.

Psychodynamics was one of the earliest schools of psychology to provide orthodox sociology with what it tended to lack: a sophisticated depth understanding of *subjectivity*, which was obviously missing in the anthropologically informed sociological theories of criminal motivation outlined above. Developing from its roots around the turn of the twentieth century, it presented social and criminological theory with a whole new dimension of thought. Very basically, in its application of Freudian and post-Freudian psychodynamic theory, criminology focused on problems that occurred in the development of the ego and super-ego. The ego is the rational part of the psyche that calculates the consequences of actions, whilst the super-ego is a combination of *conscience*, which is the producer of guilt and shame, and an identifying mechanism that connects with *ego ideals*, the symbolic figures that represent the values of the culture to which the individual belongs. As the child grows up it is vitally important that these two parts develop properly so they can deal with powerful libidinal energy produced by the id, the instinctual and unconscious third part of the psyche that seeks immediate gratification of aggressive and sexual drives. Practised in a controlled manner, these drives ensure survival and reproduction, but, practised in an uncontrolled or over-intensified manner, they can motivate the individual to perpetrate multiple harms.

The psychodynamic paradigm has been heavily criticized. In early schools of psychoanalysis mothers were often blamed for failing to perform their traditional role in helping their children to develop balanced egos and super-egos. This prompted some feminists to declare the position incorrigibly sexist, and some liberals to dismiss it as conservative, repressive and a threat to liberalism's 'life-affirming' project of emancipating the individual and its desires from restrictive norms. The importance placed by Freudians on the civilizing role of traditional institutions, such as family and work, has also been dismissed by many liberals as conservative and repressive. Some liberals are also averse to the idea that human beings are driven by powerful unconscious drives, preferring the alternative idea that we are fully conscious, rational, creative, malleable and driven by a natural sense of ethics and *élan vital* that exist prior to all social law and code (Lippens, 2012; 2013). From this elementary humanistic position we can create ourselves from scratch as sociable individuals (Lippens, 2012; 2013) and reform our laws, codes, institutions and relations in free negotiation with others in networks of communication and language (Habermas, 1984).

On the other hand, conservative criminologists are critical of the radical schools of psychoanalysis that developed in the post-1945 period, often in conjunction with Marxism, for instance the Frankfurt School (see Wiggershaus, 2010). These schools criticized capitalism's traditional institutions and popular culture for failing to develop the ego and super-ego in ways that ensure civilized values and sociable individuals, producing instead narcissistic, selfish and punitive individuals with a penchant for authoritarianism. Frankfurt School psychoanalysts such as Marcuse (1987) reminded us that Freud was well aware of *reaction-formation* as the deleterious result of excessive repression bearing down on individuals. Thus, on the whole, psychoanalysis pleases neither conservatives nor liberals, and, apart from a few interesting applications in subcultural theory, it has been largely neglected or in some cases actively discarded by the theoretical schools that have made up post-war criminology's dominant conservative and liberal wings. However, psychodynamic theory is diverse and complex; later in the book we will argue that contemporary developments in the field are very important and therefore it should be revisited by criminologists looking for a new realism in criminological theory.

Schools of sociology, psychology and social psychology proliferated in the twentieth century. Criminological theorists adapted and applied many of the new ideas emerging at the time to their task of explaining 'criminal behaviour'. Behaviourist psychologists following Skinner (1971) argued that the individual can be conditioned by prolonged exposure to a system of rewards and punishments, which eventually can be anticipated by the individual. As the individual learns to anticipate rewards and punishments she constructs an internal emotional control system in a process of 'operant conditioning'. This position is seriously flawed. The principal flaw is that mediating factors which exist between the individual and the environment – culture, ideology, traumatic memories, varying socioeconomic conditions and so on – are largely absent from the theory. It proposes that children can be trained rather like dogs, and has sunk into obsolescence, largely on the back of evidence that proved the inefficacy of behaviourist regimes in prisons and various treatment centres. Individuals tended to stick to the regime in the institutions for the sake of the rewards but behaved differently once outside, which suggests that no actual conditioning took place. Except in the most banal and specific situations, such as learning to slow down near speed cameras, this attempt to base a theory on a very simplified and mechanistic ontology of the human being was a failure.

Cognitive learning theory (or social learning theory) is far more sophisticated and contextualized. This theory is built on the principle of 'dual psychology'. Human beings, unsure of their identities, create their own meanings as they experience life and try to solve the problems it throws up, but 'significant others' in the social world intervene as individuals build their cognitive maps and identities. This basic principle comes from the psychological theory of G.H. Mead (1934) combined with American pragmatist philosophy, which views individuals as conscious problem-solvers (see Melossi, 2008). It is the psychological basis of the sociological school of symbolic interactionism and the criminological schools of differential association and subculture. However, it is still highly problematic as an explanation for why individuals or groups commit crime and harm. First, there is too much variation in the tendency to commit crimes amongst individuals exposed to the same cultural meaning-systems and influenced by the same authority figures who act as significant others. Second, and conversely, individuals exposed to different meaning-systems and influenced by different significant others can sometimes become involved in the same criminal activities, for instance the rioters in London in 2011, many of whom were 'caught up in the moment'.

The theory of *differential association*, whose main architect was Edwin Sutherland (1947), followed on from the symbolic interactionist and cultural pluralist models to consolidate them in the late 1940s and provide an alternative to strain theory. This theory proposed that criminality is not simply the expression of mainstream needs and values. Sutherland claimed that crime-prone social groups were not disorganized but 'differentially organized', which, again, softened the critique of marginalized cultures and their everyday practices and encouraged appreciative studies. However, he did admit that some subcultural value systems were oriented to criminality, and in doing so provided a bridge between the Chicago School and later subcultural theories. Individuals who have too much contact with these subcultures will learn their values and rationalizations, which can be difficult to shift if young people develop a sense of belonging and allegiance to them. Criminal traditions can therefore be reproduced as 'folkways', even though their original causes can be either non-existent or forgotten. Sutherland was one of the first to claim that subcultures in the higher echelons of society could also adopt and reproduce criminal values and practices, and thus made an inaugural and seminal contribution to the study of the 'crimes of the powerful'.

Although differential association is one of the most enduring theories it is also one of the most flawed. The theory is dependent on cognitive and social learning theory, and suffers from similar problems. In addition, the fundamental contradiction in Sutherland's theory is that he supports a pluralist model of society yet he uses a standard legal notion of 'crime' based on mainstream values and institutions, and thus carrying with it mainstream moral condemnation. The theory cannot explain crimes committed by solitary individuals and it cannot explain the original psychological, cultural, social or economic motivations for criminality or the origins of criminal subcultures. Moreover, it virtually ignores deep human drives and structural relations of class, race and gender, and it shows little awareness of the criminogenic conditions at the heart of capitalist societies. In a nutshell, it is a form of cultural reductionism, which explains the existence and reproduction of human motivations as values, norms and justifications that are learnt by individuals in distinct subcultural groups. Everything that can challenge the founding principles of cultural pluralism and social learning – consensual values and norms, ideology, abusive childhood experiences, unconscious drives, political solidarity, socioeconomic structures, social disruption caused by economic restructuring and so on – is marginalized or ignored. Sutherland, having been one of the first to point out white-collar crime, failed to follow up his own clue and look for consensual and potentially criminogenic values and desires that are shared by all groups in society and run deeper than explicit cultural meanings. Where Merton over-naturalized and homogenized values and desires, Sutherland over-culturalized, pluralized and cognitized them.

All cultural pluralist theories, such as phenomenology and symbolic interactionism, which are based on learnt cognitive meanings, overstate the individual's ability to create and negotiate 'meaningful meanings' – in other words meanings that elicit deep emotional commitment and create desires. Therefore they overestimate the depth and real difference of plural subcultural meanings in comparison to mainstream meanings. Overt communicative meanings can be rather superficial, hiding rather than revealing deep drives and desires, therefore these theories cannot account for the way in which dominant values and ideologies that pre-exist individuals and surround them as they grow up are adopted emotionally to meld with internal drives in the unconscious neurological system. These drives remain hidden but shape the desires that underlie and influence the ostensible meanings that are communicated in groups. Symbolic interactionism ignores the way that the individual's experiences of reality – for instance, abuse or neglect in childhood or negative experiences with hostile peers in adolescence – can be inscribed in the neurological system. Later, we will investigate how these two factors of *ideology* and *experience* combine when we look at *transcendental materialism*. If sufficiently powerful, emotional drives and desires can motivate the individual to bypass norms, rules, rational calculation, language and communication to simply *act out* their feelings in the real world.

Conservative control theory reversed the fundamental criminological question. Instead of asking why people commit crime, it asked why people *do not* commit crime. Conservative theorists, drawing on philosophers such as Hobbes (1996), argue that individuals are innately insecure and suffer from the 'malady of infinite aspiration'. No matter what we've got and what we've experienced, we want more, and some will bend or break the rules to get it. Such 'wicked' individuals require careful socialization and discipline by traditional institutions such as the family and the church, so they can learn to repress this impulsive drive and act towards others in a controlled, civilized manner. According to Hirschi (1969), individuals must be encouraged to develop deep sentiments of attachment, commitment, involvement and belief in their relation to these institutions, otherwise socialization will be difficult and crime and delinquency more likely. Only commitment to traditional institutions and ethico-social standards will deliver us from evil.

For radical liberals, the conservative position is anathema. It is flawed because it denies the whole idea of personal liberation and favours conformity and a nostalgic yearning for obsolete, rigid and largely oppressive traditions and institutions. However, control theory did briefly display a progressive dimension. Sykes and Matza (1957) argued that most individuals have a sense of right and wrong, but merely 'drift' into delinquency during adolescence, using 'techniques of neutralization' to justify their behaviour, and drift back out again as they grow up and controls come back into play. However, this is not in itself a theory because it offers no explanation of why only *some* young people living in similarly difficult circumstances commit crime in the first place. A more forceful critique of the conservative position is that society's traditional institutions actively reproduce an unequal class society and are sometimes themselves corrupt – for instance most sexual abuse occurs in the family, and the recent high-profile scandals in the Catholic Church and the British Broadcasting Corporation add weight to this criticism. However, later in this book we will argue that conservative control theory's main flaw is its central assumption of the 'malady of infinite aspiration' as a natural, timeless aspect of the human condition – in everyday language, it is 'just human nature', and some are more human – read 'evil' – than others.

Where radical liberals deny the existence of this unconscious drive, conservatives tell us that it is natural, a timeless 'predisposition', present to a greater degree in some individuals than in others, as we will find out now as we briefly outline contemporary biosocial theories.

Contemporary biosocial theories represent an attempt to move beyond early biological theories of criminality, which were reductive, individualistic, decontextualized, misleading and politically dangerous. Many amongst the first wave of bio-criminologists in the late nineteenth century believed that criminals lose out in society simply because they are intellectually and morally inferior. These ne'er-do-wells won't work, they don't respect authority or the rights and property of others and they turn to crime as a first resort. This aggregative notion of society and economy, which puts the individual first in the causal chain, blames the victims of unequal societies and explains lack of success and criminality in terms of natural inferiority. This sort of thinking led to the horrific politics of eugenics, whose advocates were convinced that societies could be made healthier by eliminating individuals and groups whose moral and intellectual inferiority were passed on through the generations by their genes. However, as we have already noted with the work of Ferri (1898), other biosocial theorists have argued that individual traits are not simply internal biological impulses unaffected by the external environment and inherited across generations; genetic traits do not predestine individuals to rigid patterns of behaviour. Some 'epigenetic' theories focus on genetic commands, going so far as to argue that environmental conditions can 'switch on' various genes that would otherwise remain dormant (Bird 2007; Owen 2012), whilst others focus on how neurochemicals and hormones act as mediators between the interior biological and exterior social, cultural and economic worlds (see Walsh and Beaver, 2009).

However, only some individuals exposed to similar cultural and environmental conditions commit crime or practise other forms of anti-social activity. Therefore, despite the diversity of new biosocial theories and their various attempts to connect genetic and neurological systems to external cultural and environmental factors, all these theories fall back by default on the principle of *internal predispositions*. In other words, no matter how hard they try and how sophisticated they become, biosocial theories cannot escape their basic ontological assumption that some individuals carry inside them an inbuilt tendency to do bad things.

Biosocial theorists, for instance, leave themselves with little choice but to fall back on predisposition models to explain why some rich and powerful individuals do very bad things – cheating, lying, stealing, using intimidation or violence – despite *not* existing in difficult, pressing or traumatic circumstances. Despite the claim to open scientific enquiry, there is an inbuilt conservative bias in all biosocial theories. Whether they focus on self-control or social control, biosocial theories automatically follow the conservative assumption that there is something *innately and timelessly dangerous* about human drives that must somehow be controlled by society's traditional institutions.

Overall, no matter how sophisticated and environmentally aware they have become, biosocial theories still suffer from an underlying determinism, reductionism and conservative political bias. They also depict individuals who break the law as somehow different from the rest of humanity, and different at the fundamental biological level of *predisposition*, which is not only wrong as a basis for scientific theory but still highly dangerous at the political level. Modern biosocial theorists may not argue for the elimination of 'inferior' individuals or groups by sterilization, execution or genocide, but they still tend to argue, as Walsh (2009) does, for the identification of inherently problematic individuals and their control by supposedly more sophisticated and 'humane' medical means. The only progressive outcome of this set of theories is that they can perhaps add some scientific weight to the argument for early intervention in the environments of children suffering forms of impoverishment, abuse or trauma. There is, however, a way out of these scientific and political problems, which we will encounter later when we investigate the theories of *pseudo-pacification* and *transcendental materialism*.

In the meantime, conservative control theory was undergoing major changes. In the 1980s and 1990s, one of the main architects of conservative control theory, Travis Hirschi, abandoned the idea that permanent bonding to a stable society is needed to produce socialized, law-abiding individuals. Working with Michael Gottfredson (1990), he retained the notion that crime and delinquency are the products of low impulse-control, but argued that adequate self-control can be learnt and internalized in the individual psyche during early socialization in the family. This is a subtle shift from a conservative to a more classical liberal and at times existential view of human nature, an indication of how some conservatives were becoming resigned to the inevitable dissolution of their traditional society as deindustrialization, increased geographical mobility, cultural transformation and developments in mass communication systems made traditional communities and stable societies more difficult to maintain. Individuals and nuclear families must accept the responsibility to create their own stable social bonds as they negotiate rapid and inevitable socioeconomic change. This opened up an intense debate in the control theory camp. Hagan (1989) argued that socialization of boys into risk in patriarchal households is more important. Tittle (1995) argued that the balance between control exerted and control imposed on the individual is vital; the individual needs a balance of control because a surfeit of either type – too much repression or too much autonomy – can be criminogenic. The former tends to cause submission and decadence whilst the latter tends to cause autonomy and predation. Colvin (2000) focused on coercive control as a behaviour learnt by individuals brought up in harsh family regimes, who subsequently grow up to idealize coercion as the best way to control environments in their own interests.

The problem with this overall position is that it decontextualizes the family. Other institutions should also be involved in socialization, and if we take this further, perhaps the whole society should be too, providing both material support and stability alongside ethical affirmation for the values the family is attempting to reproduce. We will see that this is not the case when we investigate the notion of *pseudo-pacification*, a concept that explains how capitalist culture stimulates and pacifies the urge for immediate gratification in order to generate amongst individuals the desire for consumer objects, which feeds into market demand and economic growth. Why some people are happy to lose themselves in consumer fantasies whilst others are driven to *act out* acquisitive and expressive urges in reality in the form of harmful crime is not explained by control theory. Colvin's theory is somewhat convincing if rather obvious, but the vital factor it does not explain is how coercion is structured into capitalism's socioeconomic world as a normal and highly functional practice in many environments ranging from criminal markets to corporate workplaces and international politics. Therefore coercion is reproduced externally in many 'normal' institutions, in which coercive actors achieve high status and rewards.

Some radical liberals, Marxists, feminists and conflict theorists argue that the family and other traditional institutions are not benign vehicles of socialization but instruments of oppression that reproduce traditional ideology, abuse and label individuals, and make life worse for children. Both positions lack nuance and context. Conservatives fail to answer the crucial contextual question of whether stability and inclusivity is possible in a divisive and culturally overheated late-capitalist society, whilst radical liberals simply call for more freedom and autonomy without bothering to address the nature of contemporary subjectivity – which types of people, with which types of desires and goals, are we setting free? As R.H. Tawney (1964) once remarked, 'freedom for the pike is death for the minnow'. The libertarian freedoms arranged on behalf of individual entrepreneurs over the past thirty-five years, for instance, have resulted in a global oligarchy (Gilens and Page, 2014) and the most unequal societies we have seen since the Gilded Age (Winlow and Hall, 2013). Late capitalism's explosion of negative freedom – i.e. freedom from restraint – has opened Pandora's Box to unleash a constellation of benign and predatory positive freedoms. Fixated on the benign forms, liberalism either denies or is intellectually ill-equipped to understand the predatory forms.

Although conservative control theory is still influential in mainstream criminology, from the 1980s onwards the political and cultural forces that became dominant in the neoliberal era of marketization, deregulation, deindustrialization and social disruption adopted a criminological school of thought much closer to their heart. Neoclassical (or right realist) theories were based firmly in the classical liberal and utilitarian philosophy that, as we have just seen, ailing traditional conservative control theory rather unsuccessfully tried to adopt. This position regards crime as simply evil done by evil-doers who choose to break a democratic society's consensual laws. Apart from a few concessions given to mental health issues and truly abject situational circumstances, any investigation into underlying causes is fruitless. The government must construct an efficient criminal justice system that will implant the idea of the certainty of arrest and punishment in the minds of potential offenders. The costs of offending must always outweigh the benefits of offending in the realms of perception and reality. However, in the 1970s the death penalty and a relatively high imprisonment rate already existed in the USA, which led J.Q. Wilson (1975) to suggest that an increase in the *efficiency* of the justice system, rather than its *harshness*, was the way forward.

A number of strategies grew out of this way of thinking, including the 'broken windows' thesis, enhanced surveillance systems, situational crime prevention, target hardening, routine activities theory, securitization and 'experimental criminology'. All these strategies were attempts to find ways of deterring, diverting and incapacitating criminals. Of all the schools of criminology, this one has probably exerted the most influence on US and UK governments in the neoliberal era. Neoclassicism's advocates openly celebrate their renunciation of sociological or psychological explanations of crime causation. They advocate a technical approach to 'securitization' rather than a critical and politically interventionist approach to causality and social reaction, which suggests that this position and its technocratic offshoots do not deserve the title 'theory' at all. Even though neoclassicism can contribute to the temporary situational reduction of crime rates, it is apolitical, unable to offer crime-ridden communities an enduring progressive move away from their problems, and willing to serve any form of government that happens to be in office. Furthermore, right realism seems to be largely uninterested in recognizing, exposing and reducing the systematic crimes of the powerful.

However, rising crime rates in Britain and the USA up to the mid-1990s demonstrated that neoclassicism was initially ineffective in its principal aim of deterring crime. It could be argued that when it became more developed it had a significant impact on the statistical crime decline that occurred from the mid-1990s until the late 2000s, but, as we shall see later, it is more likely that securitization forced crime not to decline but to *mutate* into more sophisticated and less detectable forms (Kotze and Temple, 2014). It could also be argued in zemiological terms that the insidious harms inflicted on society by intensive securitization and incarceration in many ways outweigh the harms caused by street crime. Overall, because it dismisses any scientific or philosophical inquiry into the underlying economic, social, cultural and psychological conditions that promote crime, and it is extremely reluctant to broaden its vision from the narrow socio-legal construction of 'crime' to the ontological concept of harm, this position can be regarded as an *anti-theory* that has obstructed rather than helped the development of criminology's theoretical project. Even conservative control theory had something to say about social bonds and how they help the formation of civilized character traits, and thus had more to offer than right realism.

Social structure and social learning theory attempted to reintroduce the underlying social context that had been neglected by neoclassicism and, to a large extent, by other mainstream positions such as developmental psychology and life-course theory (see for example Moffitt, 1993). Based on the notion, first introduced to criminology by Edwin Sutherland (1947), that individuals do not merely *associate* with others in a cultural or subcultural group but *learn* their values, behaviours and justifications from dominant individuals within it, this perspective tries to place this basic notion in a structural context. Deviant associations and the dominance of deviant definitions in the group actually cause and reproduce criminality or delinquency – there is no need for antecedent causes in the real external socioeconomic world or in unconscious drives. Akers (1998) places this cultural theory, again based on meanings and definitions, in a social-structural context; in other words gender, class, age and how well 'organized' the community is tend to be important variables that influence whether criminal or delinquent meanings will be learnt, normalized, justified and reproduced over time. The basic premise is that social learning mediates the effects of these structural variables on individual behaviour. The main point for policymakers is that whatever is learnt can be unlearnt, even though meanings can be difficult to shift as individuals become committed to them and subcultural groups coalesce around them.

This theory is a development of the phenomenologically-based positions of symbolic interactionism, social learning theory and differential association theory, and suffers from the same problems. There are no explanations for crimes committed by isolated individuals, the motivations behind specific acts or why some young people drift into criminal or delinquent groups and others from the same family or background do not. It cannot explain why the existence of these groups varies in different historical periods and social spaces. It cannot explain why some individuals from a similar location in the social structure and from a similar cultural background do not follow or interpret cultural meanings in the same way. Conversely, it cannot explain why people from very different backgrounds commit crimes and engage in anti-social activities. The problem here is that, like all interpretivist learning theories, this one is based on a notion of *positive ideology* as an aspect of consciousness; in other words individuals' ideas and actions are the products of knowledge picked up in association with others. As we shall see in more detail later, the culture that attends liberal-postmodern capitalism is based on the *negative ideology* of capitalist realism, which creates space for the disavowed and therefore unconscious adoption of the aggressive dispositions that life in a competitive individualist culture demands. All 'subcultures', no matter how exotic and diverse they might seem on the surface, are variations of this dominant competitive form (see Redhead, 2014), in which aggressive, anti-social activities are normal and distinguished only by differences in scale, situation and degree of sublimation.

By ignoring the dominant competitive-aggressive cultural form and focusing on the intersection of social-structural relations in communities, and suggesting that the community has the ability to deal with these antagonistic relations, social structure and social learning theory restricts criminology's vision to the mid-range and assumes that communities have enough influence and solidarity to reorganize these relations. In other words the small community, not the broader society and its politics and culture, becomes the site of social reproduction and justice, and the focus of cultural and pedagogical intervention – little shelters in the storm where capitalism's fundamental antagonisms, desires and drives can be 'learnt' and 'unlearnt'. As we shall see later when we encounter critical realism and transcendental materialism, social structure and social learning theory is one of many mainstream theories that perform the important political task of discouraging the notion that political intervention is required at a *deeper level* in the socioeconomic structure and its attendant consumer culture. In other words, by focusing on the cultural effects of various social axes at the points they intersect rather than the structure itself along with its underlying ideology, values, desires and drives, it is yet another form of biopolitics operating in the post-political world.

3

THE CRITICAL TRADITION

In the late nineteenth and early twentieth centuries, European socialist and communist thinkers associated criminality with powerful economic and cultural forces and social injustices that are intrinsic to the capitalist system. Thinkers such as Engels (1987), Bonger (1916) and Tawney (1964) argued that capitalism's antagonistic class-structured social system will always alienate unemployed, precarious and low-paid workers, throwing many into poverty and immiseration. Capitalist culture is based on the principle of competitive individualism, which impedes the working-class solidarity project by fostering egotism and competitiveness amongst the population. As people compete against each other some break the ethical codes and rules that hold communities together, thus 'demoralizing' society and increasing crime and other forms of anti-social behaviour.

Bonger (ibid.) was aware that the relationship between individuals and their material conditions of living is always mediated by culture. His main point was that those amongst the poor who lack a cultural awareness of the need for social and political solidarity in their situation of adversity are more likely to commit crime and engage in other forms of anti-social activity. Marx and Engels (1972) had categorized working-class individuals who refuse to recognize their mutual class interests as the 'lumpenproletariat', a group with a tendency to selfishness, reactionary politics and criminality.

However, as capitalism developed over the twentieth century, wages increased and, on average, most workers actually became wealthier. Crime increased statistically in both Britain and the USA, slowly after the First World War but quite rapidly from the late 1960s onwards (Reiner, 2007). Some wealthy individuals commit crime, risk harming others and take part in immoral activities in order to become even wealthier or wield power over others, so the link between poverty and demoralization is very tenuous. Other socialists and Marxists noticed that despite poverty, hardship and a dominant culture of competitive individualism, some working-class communities retained solidarity, sought political solutions to their problems and did not become 'demoralized' or descend into criminality (see Williams, 1971).

However, some individuals did, but there has been a tendency in radical criminology to reject the issue of immorality and its link to criminality. Radical criminologists prefer to see most of the crimes of the powerless as 'social crimes' – rational and justifiable responses to oppression, injustice and socioeconomic exclusion – whilst the crimes of the powerful are expressions of opportunism and domination amongst the elite. Conservatives, on the other hand, regard the tendency to immorality as the timeless ontological core of the human condition in the secular world of sinners, against which the individual and all social institutions must struggle. Those who succumb to immorality will descend in the social order because they are untrustworthy and dysfunctional. We will see later, when we move beyond critical realism to *transcendental materialism* and *pseudo-pacification*, that neither of these positions, nor indeed any hybrid positions drawn from them, are tenable as plausible explanations of crime and harm.

We can see clearly that both socialists and conservatives had few problems with the notions of a dominant ideology and a 'hegemonic' culture. However, a little later in the twentieth century, in the inter-war years, radical momentum was generated in a liberal-progressive direction when US Chicago School sociologists rejected European socialist ideas. They also moved away from the dominant 'soft conservative' Durkheimian position, which argued that a cultural and moral consensus – a broad agreement on what is right and wrong about life – exists at the core of society. Sociology, as we have seen, moved in the direction of *cultural pluralism*. The pluralist position is based on the principle that there is no dominant way of life and a cultural and moral diversity exists at the core of all societies. In other words, the bedrock of 'society' consists of a number of different cultural groups and individuals who harbour different moral principles and views on what is right and wrong, and have different sets of norms and rules for organizing themselves as groups. This position insisted that we should understand and appreciate rather than criticize or pathologize different ways of life, a principle that was behind a plethora of ethnographic studies that set out to appreciate different cultures and subcultures, or at least balance criticism with appreciation.

This appreciative pluralist position was clearly motivated by ethics and politics rather than social scientific analysis. It was partly a reaction against the terrible things that were being done to people whose cultures were seen as pathological and thus a threat to the mainstream consensus. We must conclude that the pluralist position became dominant in twentieth century sociology and criminology not because of the strength of its underlying theoretical principles but because it led us away from the brutal twentieth century political manifestations of pathologization such as Nazism and Stalinism by insisting on inter-cultural appreciation and tolerance (see Rafter, 2009).

Although this fear of authoritarian social reaction was proven to be well-founded, and the appreciative principle was appropriate in the study of peripheral crimes such as delinquency, drug-taking and prostitution, it has little to offer criminology's attempt to theorize serious consensual crimes such as murder, rape, assault and extortion committed by individuals and both state and non-state organizations. It has little conception of structural class, race and gender relations and it seems suspicious of the notion that collective ethics and politics can transcend and create solidarity amongst plural cultures to fight socioeconomic inequality. It also assumes a diversity of ends rather than means when in fact a significant majority of individuals and cultural groups in modern consumer-capitalist societies share a common end – to 'make it' by becoming financially successful and acquiring conventional symbols of social status such as expensive cars and houses – but disagree about what are 'fair' and 'legal' means to achieve this end (Hall, 2012a).

Early US subcultural theories followed on from diffe   .
theory, and suffered from the same flaws, especially
'enclosed meaning'. Was US society totally plural ri,
roots and were subcultures separatist in the sense of bein
able to reproduce their intrinsically different values, norm ....u meanings
uninfluenced by society's dominant cultural meanings? Albert Cohen
(1955) did not think so. He argued that although mainstream values
cannot be imposed directly on individuals, they can be partially accepted
and reworked by subcultural groups who cannot completely escape the
powerful influence they exert on the structures, institutions, norms,
unconscious drives/desires and practices of the society in which they
live. We will see later, when we draw upon the works of Slavoj Žižek,
that it is not necessary for individuals to learn and positively believe in
society's core values but only to *act as if they do* – because they *negatively*
believe no alternative is possible – for a dominant ideology and socioeconomic logic to continue to reproduce themselves over a long period
of time. Thus 'subcultures' might well create various hybrids of values,
norms and meanings, sometimes inverting them, sometimes practising
them in extreme or malicious ways and sometimes directly opposing them
'just for kicks', but none of this has any impact on the capitalist system's
reproductive momentum (Miles, 2014; Buccellato and Reid, 2014).

Cloward and Ohlin (1960) argued that criminal and delinquent
values are more likely to be practised in economically poor areas where
access to delinquent opportunities is easy in the 'neighbourhood milieu'.
Subcultures specialize in various ways around the following core activities:
organized criminal practice usually for financial gain; disorganized conflictual practice such as violence or vandalism; and retreatist practice
such as drug use. However, the specialist tendency has now virtually
disappeared to be replaced by all-purpose economically-orientated scaven-
ging and opportunist violence (Soothill et al., 2008), which is rendering
traditional subcultural theory obsolete (Hobbs, 2013; Redhead, 2014)
and adding weight to Žižek's claim that 'plural' values do not drive or
shape socioeconomic action. Any genuine plurality tends to appear on
the plane of norms and rules, which offer different means – or 'strategic
normative practices' – to similar ends (Hall et al., 2008).

Classic subcultural theories also over-predict crime amongst the
powerless and ignore criminality and harmful activity amongst the

powerful in society; white-collar, governmental and state crimes. There are also many indications that so-called oppositional subcultures have conformist and authoritarian – in some cases almost paramilitary – modes of organization (see Downes, 1966; Pitts, 2008), and that most youth groups are very mundane and mainstream, whereas the 'zookeepers' of subcultural theory select only the exotic types (see Gouldner, 1973). The US theorist David Matza (1964) entered the argument in the early 1960s by stressing that young people's membership of criminal or delinquent subcultures was temporary; on the whole they tended to drift in during their teenage years and drift out during their mid-twenties when they rejoined the mainstream by getting jobs, getting married and having children. At the time Matza probably had a point, but today, in the postindustrial consumer era, when those traditional transitions into adulthood have collapsed in an infantilized 'adultescent' culture (see Hayward, 2012a; Smith, 2014), or in many deindustrialized and poor areas where most work is part-time, temporary and precarious, his theory appears to be rather dated.

Despite these obvious flaws, the cultural pluralist paradigm received another major boost in the 1960s as interpretivism, symbolic inter-actionism and labelling theory became more influential. The root of this school of thought is *phenomenology*, the philosophical position based on the principle that 'phenomena' – or the way things appear in the world – are consciously interpreted by individuals, but interpreted differently by different people. The essential nature of things, what the philosopher Kant called 'noumena', can never be fully understood, therefore we can forget about trying to establish objective 'truths' in the external world. People interpret what they encounter in the world by using their existing stocks of knowledge, their personal experiences and their interests. Thus we can understand crime only by getting down into the immediate personal worlds of criminals and victims to gather their unique interpretations.

However, the New York school of phenomenology argued that powerful social groups can impose their meanings on others. This was also the basis of symbolic interactionism, which takes up G.H. Mead's (1934) principle that, as the individual interprets phenomena by having an internal conversation between the 'I' and the 'me', 'significant others' – which means authority figures in the external social world – intrude in the conversation and influence the way the individual constructs meaning and interprets phenomena. Labelling theory followed on from that principle, arguing that powerful social groups interpret criminal actions in the way that suits them, and impose these dominant meanings – usually prejudiced and condemnatory – on those who commit criminal acts. Therefore, some young people who are unsure of their identity and commit minor crimes accept the imposed label 'criminal' as part of their identity, which encourages the escalation and reproduction of criminal activity. Meanwhile, the public also accept this dominant meaning, which encourages a harsh social reaction and unnecessarily hauls the young person into the criminal justice system, further alienating the young person from mainstream society and causing further or 'secondary' criminal deviation from society's norms. British theorists called this process 'deviancy amplification spirals' (Wilkins, 2001). 'Deviance' or 'crime' have no essential ontological truth; they are simply words, labels slapped on young people by powerful rule-making groups in order to demonize them and gloss over the problems experienced by young people as they struggle to obtain a foothold in a competitive society and an unstable economy. This overall position was a strong advocate for minimal intervention by criminal justice systems in young people's lives.

Although this position was highly influential in the latter half of the twentieth century, it has numerous flaws. First, phenomenology is a dubious philosophical position. Often used by interpretivist social scientists as an antidote to crude positivist analyses that claim to pinpoint the 'real objective causes' of crime in the external world, phenomenology swings the pendulum too far in the opposite direction. It claims that we can know very little about the underlying nature and systemic causes of phenomena in the external world apart from other people's interpretations of them. Second, do individuals stop to interpret phenomena consciously before they act or react to other people's actions? Perhaps not. In the world of interpretivism and phenomenology, everything – crime, harm, drive, motivation, conditions – becomes merely an interpretation and a label constructed by some group or other for their own interests. Presumably, we cannot know anything certain about these 'groups' or their 'interests', because they too are only labels. Thus, the fundamental flaw is 'infinite regression' – each attempt to establish what words might refer to in the external world is denied and turned back in on itself, which traps us in a process of asking endless questions as we 'negotiate' what things are and what things mean, none of which can ever be properly answered. To negotiate meaning with others is perhaps a good thing working in the interests of democracy, but to be unable ever to reach any firm conclusions means that, apart from freeing people from unfair labels, we can never really know anything for sure, which in turn means that we can never be sure how to act positively and politically in the world to transform anything for the better.

To explain the influence of mainstream meanings, Lemert (1974), along with others such as Howard Becker (1963), also turned to symbolic interactionism and labelling theory but emphasized the notions of autonomy and resistance. The basic idea that young people were not part of an integrated mainstream, and they were in some way creating alternative meanings in order to 'resist' the authority of the mainstream, crossed the Atlantic to influence British thinking. In his study *The Delinquent Solution* (1966), British criminologist David Downes rejected subcultural theories based on either strain theory or pure interpretivist and pluralist principles. He brought history and long-term cultural reproduction back into the equation by arguing that young British men relied on their own traditional 'tough' values as they tried to deal with structural problems such as unemployment.

Members of the Birmingham School of Contemporary Cultural Studies partially agreed with the notion of continuity but took a tangential direction, arguing that many young working-class people involved in subcultures were not reworking traditional values to *integrate* with mainstream conservative society but to *resist* it, but their oppositional stance to the state, the ruling class and the mainstream media was 'imaginary' rather than real. For Phil Cohen (1972), traditional Puritan working-class values were clashing with the hedonistic values of consumer culture that had become dominant in the post-war era. Overall, the British theorists placed subculture in a structural context that emphasized class struggle, looking at how various subcultural groups dealt with their subordinate socioeconomic class position and 'resisted' and 'reworked' the values and meanings the elite tried to impose on them (Hebdige, 1979).

However, after unwisely ignoring the integrationist element of Downes' earlier study, the British subcultural paradigm became a morass of unfounded assumptions based on an overarching romantic view of young people. The fundamental assumption was that, historically, young working-class 'Puritans' were somehow resisting the hedonistic values and meanings that the mass media and consumer culture had been promoting since the 1950s. As we shall see later when we discuss consumer culture, nothing could be further from the truth. This theory was a child of the 'new left', a broader movement we criticize in detail elsewhere (Winlow et al., 2015). It was based on British historian E.P. Thompson's (1971) notion of the 'moral economy', a long-running organic English working-class culture of ethico-political resistance against the ruling class and the state. In reality this resistance was sporadic and fragmented across British history, existing in organized forms only in the industrial heyday. The British working class never became a unified 'proletariat', an ethically and politically driven 'class for itself'. Thompson did not agree with the counterculture's libertarian hedonism that was crossing the Atlantic into Europe in the 1960s, but he appealed to its romanticism in order to dismiss the important question that had been asked by more serious philosophical thinkers such as Gramsci (1971) and Althusser (1969): why do so many working-class people, like turkeys voting for Christmas, reproduce the ideology of the system that exploits, oppresses and, latterly, economically excludes them and systematically destroys their political and social worlds (see also Winlow and Hall, 2013)?

The dismal reality is that, as alternative sources of identity recede into history, most young working-class people *actively seek* their incorporation into consumer culture, which promotes capitalism's dominant ideology and cynically uses young people's propensity to 'rebel' against their parents for commercial purposes (Heath and Potter, 2006; Hall et al., 2008; Miles, 2014; Buccellato and Reid, 2014). This fundamental error, rooted in a romantic middle-class fantasy of the working class rather than a serious analysis or an experiential self-definition, has been carried forward and still acts as a dominant and very misleading – we might even say intellectually and politically catastrophic – principle in today's sociological and criminological theories of youth and crime. Resistance against the system was not even 'imaginary', it simply did not exist in any ideational or political form apart from the easily incorporated and commercialized rebellion against older generations. The irony – indeed the tragedy – is that these older generations had contained some individuals who had been far more dangerous political radicals than countercultural youth, and who had sustained and practised radical politics far more effectively in the decades preceding the so-called 'radical' 1960s. Rebelling against your mum, your dad, your record collection and your wardrobe and having lots of mischievous fun is not the same as resisting capitalism. In fact capitalism captured young people's hearts and minds by affirming and assisting their rebellion against their parents at the same time as conveniently selling them the symbolic goods – clothes, pop records and so on – they needed to do so (Heath and Potter, 2006; Smith, 2014). Young people in the 1960s were not 'rebels without a cause', they were rebels unwittingly fighting for the cause of post-politics, rapidly discarding their coherent political symbolism and dissipating their political unconscious as they were absorbed into the endless mission of gratifying consumer desires by acquiring and displaying consumer symbols. From the 1960s onwards, apart from a tiny few fringe activists, youth culture was politically sterilized.

Recruiting dissenters who were critical of capitalism but even more critical of the horrors and failures of state socialism in the mid-twentieth century, the faux-radical juggernaut inspired by 'new left' cultural Marxism (see Dworkin, 1997) gathered significant mass and momentum. It inspired the 'new criminology', which, outlined in a book of the same name (Taylor et al., 1973) argued for a 'fully social theory of deviance'. This looked promising because it combined an investigation into the causes of crime with an accompanying investigation of the problems associated with the often disproportionate social reaction to crime and the labelling of criminals. The investigation into causality tried to combine the broader social and economic context, the individual's culture and biography, and the micro-situation in which the crime was committed. The investigation into social reaction tried to combine the immediate reaction of the criminal justice system, such as policing practices, the broader social context (such as class, power, ideology and morality) and the outcomes of social reaction (such as labelling and deviancy amplification). Social reaction was seen as part of a 'conservative' moral climate somehow tied to political economy and the state, which normalized the repression of the individual as he or she struggled for freedom. Overall, it saw deviance as a form of misguided rebellion or 'proto-politics' and asked criminologists to look at the control system and its power to criminalize 'human diversity' as an important factor in the creation and reproduction of the material conditions and 'social arrangements' in which individuals choose to commit crime.

The authors of this hybrid symbolic interactionist and cultural Marxist position used the standard mainstream conception of deviance as an act or gesture against society's rules, rarely discussing whether they were talking about ontologically harmful or harmless forms of deviance. Relying on the flawed principle that 'crime' and 'deviance' are simply labels led the 'new criminologists' to ignore the fact that the harm caused by some forms of crime and deviance has an ontological and experiential reality insofar as they act as real forces that leave individuals and their environments worse off than they were before they were victimized (see Honneth, 1996; Hillyard et al., 2004; Yar, 2012). The 'new criminologists' also assumed that crime was a deviation from society's values and norms rather than the raw and unrefined practising of capitalist society's fetishistically disavowed central values (egotism and aggressive competition amongst individuals and companies for market share, economic wealth and social status) in ways that defy and bypass its norms (everyday ethics, rules and codes of behaviour). They completely ignored biological factors and used highly selective social psychological perspectives that followed the fashion of the time by regarding the family as an aspect of the repressive social structure that reproduced oppression and alienation. This meant that the relationship between the social totality and the individual was left relatively unexplored. The little attention they paid to social psychology revolved around the notion that capitalist societies place people in difficult circumstances which place pressure on them to *consciously choose* deviance – we will criticize this in more detail later when we find out how capitalism's culture can tap into unconscious drives.

Although the authors of *The New Criminology* (Taylor et al., 1973) offered a brief critique of social reaction theory (Chapter 5), the thesis itself ended up in the conclusion (Chapter 9) as a standard social reaction theory that offered very few insights into why capitalism's 'political economy' and 'social totality' were prone to criminality, apart from the secondary causal process of deviancy amplification caused by the repressive control system. As Horsley argues, criminological theory's main problem is that:

> [O]ur decades-long dalliance with social reaction seems to have produced little of any value when it comes to actually explaining the socio-ethical basis for criminality and the cultural ideals that apparently justify the infliction of harm in the service of instrumental or expressive interests.
>
> *(2014b: 95)*

No analysis of primary causal processes and conditions was forthcoming. The new criminology movement – whilst full of promises to explain why capitalism was criminogenic, and quite right to berate earlier US theories for focusing on subcultures without investigating the capitalist social system as a whole – failed to offer its own coherent explanation of crime and harm. Rather than attempt to integrate valuable ideas from psychoanalysis, conflict theory, strain theory and so on, it dismissed them, yet it failed to provide convincing alternatives. The authors admitted this failing in the conclusion, but left no real clues as to how future research programmes and theories might take up the call to produce a 'fully social' theory of deviance that included structure, process and culture, other than repeating *ad nauseam* the command that, whatever they come up with, it should be a 'fully social' theory of deviance that included structure, process and culture.

The New Criminology was a premature manifesto with limited scientific, philosophical or political substance. Like most criminological manifestos of this type, it told criminologists what to do without providing any coherent explanatory concepts, analyses or theoretical frameworks that might help them to do it. Instead it spent a lot of time dismissing potentially useful ideas; for instance, typical of its time, a child of the 'counterculture', it denied capitalism's tendency to produce selfish, egotistical and apolitical forms of subjectivity and misrepresented this as the individual's struggle for freedom and diversity. Basically, it failed entirely to engage with the fundamental political question of the twentieth century, which, as we have seen above, had been asked by Gramsci and Althusser, amongst others – why do most people pushed into difficult circumstances by capitalism's unfair social system continue to compete against each other rather than group together to oppose the system itself? There is no doubt that *The New Criminology* was a landmark text, but only insofar as it was a giant 'diversion' sign that ushered criminology further down an 'alternative route' round the back lanes to negative anti-realist thinking and blocked criminologists' vision from useful ideas from its past and alternative ideas emerging in its present.

In the 1970s *critical criminology* grew out of the 'new criminology' school, inaugurated by an edited collection of the same name (Taylor et al., 1975). While the conflict theorists saw social conflict as a struggle over authority by various cultural groups in a potentially democratic, harmonious and consensual society, Marxists argued that capitalist societies are inherently polarized and riven by class conflict that cannot be superseded without fundamental change. However, the critical criminologists, mindful of the violence and totalitarian bureaucracies that followed communist revolutions in the twentieth century, argued along liberal–idealist lines that this change can *only* be brought about in the dimensions of meaning, interpretation, symbolic interaction and piecemeal legal and sociocultural reform. Creating space for different meanings and understandings will lead to bottom-up democratic transformation, they promised. Their fundamental criminological argument was that most petty offenders were not committed criminals but the victims of capitalism's unequal social order. These offenders committed minor crimes to alleviate poverty, insecurity and marginalization, but the law was constructed by the ruling class to be unfairly and disproportionately focused on the offences committed by the subordinate class. This harsh attitude was supported by a mainstream culture and media that labelled petty offenders as wilful, committed criminals from an inferior and immoral culture at the very bottom of the social hierarchy. The poor and powerless were therefore punished harshly for committing minor and often victimless crimes whilst the more serious crimes of the wealthy business class and the state went unpunished.

Early critical criminology in the 1970s focused heavily on the critique of the category 'crime' as a social construction, which of course it is, or more precisely a politically-charged socio-legal construction. However, in these early days before the initial feminist intervention there was no sophisticated discussion of the ontology of harm and too little attention paid to the harmful consequences of some everyday crimes. Critical criminology's overriding notion of harm was quite basic and structural. The corporate state and its agents caused the greatest harm as they oppressed the working class and the free individual. Popular perceptions of crime were the products of a traditional fear of the 'dangerous other' stoked up by the mass media rather than a logical analysis of experiential harm and its causes. Working-class petty criminals caused a lot less harm yet they were victimized by increasingly heavy-handed criminal justice policies. This state oppression was legitimized by popular fear, and the whole process was expressed neatly in Hall's (1980) phrase, 'the drift into a law and order society'.

However, the political use of fear is significantly more complex than the critical criminologists' unidirectional structural theory suggests. Social science had placed an embargo on freethinking rational enquiry by allowing itself to be confined and driven by a dualistic and mutually reinforcing fear. The liberal left feared the barbarism of order – the state operating on behalf of the ruling class to oppress the freeborn individual – whilst the conservatives feared the barbarism of disorder – the unruly and potentially violent lower-class mob threatening the natural and functional social order. Each political group saw the other's fear as an irrational response to the benign form they regarded as necessary for a healthy, stable society (see Hall, 2012a). However, this dualistic fear was not clearly separated in the imagination of the liberal left or the liberal right. The liberal-left social reaction theory that underpinned critical criminology to spawn the rather nebulous concept of 'moral panic' was also fuelled by a poorly concealed fear of the unruly mob as well as a fear of the state (see Hall, 2012a; Thompson and Williams, 2013). The liberal right feared both, too, but their fear of the state was inclined towards its economic regulatory power rather than its social control apparatus.

When it was not presenting a one-dimensional view of the politics of fear, critical criminology sometimes expressed itself as a simple economic cost-benefit analysis. The economic 'crimes of the powerful' were costing nations up to four times as much as petty crime (Levi, 1987), whilst crimes such as the neglect of health and safety regulations caused numerous illnesses and deaths amongst employees. Therefore critical criminologists argued for a significant shift of focus onto the crimes of the powerful: governmental, corporate and white-collar crime. It also delivered a powerful political message. Not only did the constant demonization of the poor and powerless by the corporate media turn the population – including the wealthier members of the working class – against the poor, which furthered alienation, hindered solidarity and ideologically justified the state's disproportionate surveillance, criminalization and punishment of the poor, it also distracted attention from the crimes of the powerful. Critical criminology was not 'plain wrong' about this structural imbalance of political power and the disproportionate attention paid by the criminal justice system to the crimes of the poor. This is its major positive contribution to criminology, but the simplistic hypodermic 'divide and rule' explanation is something of a truism that, as we shall see later, obscures the deeper, more sophisticated and politically important analysis of ideology that explains why the poor collude in their own alienation and do not stand up to the ruling class in a more organized and effective way.

Nevertheless, critical criminology had a significant impact on the discipline. Although the normative principle of actually having a critical position within criminology is a very good one, the sub-discipline as it has developed is shot through with major problems. The British variant was more influenced by humanist and cultural Marxism, and the US version by liberalism, anarchism, feminism and left-libertarianism. Both were heavily influenced by intersectional identity politics, which placed gender and ethnic relations at the forefront of the debate and tended to obscure the fundamental social class relation. Its initial mistake was to confine aetiological investigations of criminal motivations to the parameters set by structural power relations that exist between social groups or the individual and the state, and to assume that 'power' is universally associated with 'domination'.

However, most petty crime and violent crime is intra-class, which refutes the 'structural domination' assumption and its associated theories of 'resistance'; crime is not being committed by 'the dominant' and neither is it an expression of 'resistance' against 'the dominant' or their values. Critical criminology's recent adoption of intersectionality theory, which examines the intersections of social power relations of domination and resistance along the axes of class, ethnicity, gender and age, tried to redress this problem. This fails, of course, in a post-political era where those relations, despite the gross inequality that often characterizes them, no longer exist in any real *political* sense but only in a *competitive* sense. A lot of the 'demonization' of the working class derives from members of the working class itself and the media from which they prefer to get their ideas and information. Many law-abiding working-class people would like to see a reduction of the crime they have to suffer in their neighbourhoods, even if that requires more policing and harsher sentencing. These sentiments cannot solely be the products of structural domination or ideology promoted by the mass media, the government and the criminal justice system, and must be at least partially generated by *real experience* and relatively autonomous interpretations. Structural theories that focus on what they imagine to be a political battle of ideas across the broad social structure tend to marginalize these two important factors.

Many laws exist not to legitimize structural domination but to protect vulnerable citizens in all social classes. Some critical criminologists acknowledged this problem and shifted their critique to the 'crisis of enforcement' (Tombs and Whyte, 2003), which means the difficulty the criminal justice system experiences when it uses existing laws that support the vulnerable to prosecute the powerful for the crimes they commit against workers, customers and citizens. Basically, laws exist but they are not adequately applied. However, a crucial fact that what we might call structural critical criminology tends to marginalize is that some of the crimes the poor and powerless commit are not minor; for instance murder, assault, domestic violence or selling addictive and psychoactive drugs to very young people. It's difficult to argue against the premise that the rich and powerful escape prosecution for many of their crimes by either influencing the formation of law or avoiding the enforcement of law, but to portray criminals from the subordinate classes as 'victimized actors', or innocent victims of the state and the media, flies in the face of the reality of their victims' experiences of harms (Young, 1975; Lea and Young, 1984).

Reading through the orthodox critical criminology literature, one might be forgiven for assuming that its adherents have been socialized in an environment of anti-realism, in which realism itself has become a folk-devil, associated with administrative criminology and state power. This hostility to realism has become a norm in critical criminology, yet many who work in this area demonstrate an unsophisticated understanding of realism and its variants, often conflating it with positivism (see for example Cooper, 2012).

As it stands, in its traditional structural-idealist position, critical criminology is replete with problems. First, as we have already seen, the structural model of power is too crude for criminological application.

On one hand we know that in the broader socioeconomic structure political and economic executive powers are concentrated in the ruling neoliberal business elite and the politicians who support their endeavours. However, populations keep on voting neoliberal governments of various shades into office, therefore, unfortunately, invoking Arendt's (1963) distinction, at least some portion of this 'power' is in reality *authority* in the sense that it is legitimized and authorized by the majority of the voting population. On the other hand, specifically criminological power, the ability and motivation to cause harm to others and their environments in order to further the interests of the self, can be found in diverse forms throughout the social structure from the domestic home and the street to the corporate boardroom. The elite have the ability to cause expansive harms that are damaging to large numbers of individuals and their environments, and indeed cost more in financial terms (Levi, 1987), but criminology should not understate the harms inflicted on a variety of victims and their sociocultural environments by individuals and small groups throughout the social structure (Young, 1975).

To hold to account only concentrated elite criminality and harm would be simply to lobby for a political reorganization of the socioeconomic structure. We have been there before, and, to use Orwell's famous metaphor, the pigs ended up sitting at the farmer's table. However, to hold diffuse reticular criminality and harm to account – harmful crime committed by predatory individuals to further their own instrumental or expressive interests throughout the nodes and arteries of the reticular capitalist socioeconomic system (see Hall, 2012a) – would be to hold to account not just those who dominate in the current social structure but the *whole liberal-capitalist way of life* and its core drives, dreams, desires, subjectivities and culture.

Besides, even if we accept the structural model, ignore working-class harm and focus on the crimes of the powerful and their power to punish, and cut a political strategy according to this cloth, there is little use in holding concentrated power to 'democratic account' even as an initial ideological strategy. Concentrated power *already knows the truth* and the extant and likely consequences of its actions, but it does not care, and, to hammer in this nail further, neither do the majority of the population as long as the elite promises and appears to deliver a short-term 'escape from evil' (Becker, 1975). Thus, at the moment, the shapeless and

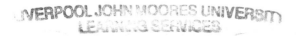

incoherent liberal left cannot drum up enough firm democratic support to make serious demands on the elite (Winlow and Hall, 2013).

Orthodox critical criminology's more recent focus on identity politics is politically divisive. The 1960s-vintage 'new left' is not only dead but it has left behind a legacy of political corrosion and exhaustion. Lazily continuing to draw upon ideas from the usual 'new left' thinkers from this bygone countercultural age (see Dworkin, 1997 for examples and a full discussion) simply demonstrates the intellectual obsolescence at the heart of the project. In the context of neoliberalism's post-social competitive-individualist culture (see Winlow and Hall, 2013), inter-sectional identity politics has had the effect of fragmenting the left's potential socialist and social democratic opposition into hostile adversaries, incorporating individuals into neoliberalism's competitive-individualist culture and postponing any new form of solidarity that might arise. Each section of the intersectional matrix has developed the habit of focusing all of its attention on demonizing and in some cases advocating the criminalization of its erstwhile oppressor. Thus, by default, each one has actively colluded in neoliberalism's ideological strategy of creating as many antagonistic sociocultural divisions as possible and distracting critical attention from the system itself and the world it is currently making for us. 'Divide and rule' is a crude and ancient political tactic, but it still seems to work quite well, and even better if the ruled do the dividing themselves.

The 'new left' paradigm suffers from the absence of a coherent critique of the capitalist system and its primary narcissistic, competitive-individualist culture (see Hall et al., 2008), but one of the few common enemies that can bring the endlessly bickering discourses of identity politics together is the corporate state. The critique of 'governmentality' – with its industrial output of endless treatises on how we are 'governed through crime' (see Simon, 2007) – and the injunction to focus primarily on 'state harms' easily degenerates into a crude anti-statism and fixes our political focus on the inert, undialectical state–individual relation (Bosteels, 2010; Jameson, 2010). Thus we tend to forget that the 'state of exception', Carl Schmitt's justification of the state's ability to declare an emergency, suspend civil rights and use violence against individuals with impunity (see Agamben, 2005), also serves powerful individuals and private organizations on whose behalf the state acts (Hall and Winlow, 2003;

Hall, 2012a). Criminology should continue to reveal and analyse state crimes but, without degenerating into grand conspiracy theory, it should also look at who and what is behind the state.

Influential anti-statist elements in critical criminology clash badly with those who advocate the crisis of enforcement argument. This also creates the sort of internal contradiction and confusion that discredits critical criminology and reminds us all that the current liberal left is mired in the symbolic inefficiency of *metanoia*, a constant mind in crisis. For instance, in the inaugural edition of the left-liberal journal *Radical Criminology*, a rather feisty editorial that demonizes the state (Shantz, 2012) is followed immediately by an article which points out that Mexico suffers from high rates of violent crime because the state has failed (Kienscherf, 2012). Perhaps the protection of the public requires a democratic state to regulate the activity of Tawney's (1964) 'free pikes' as they move in to kill the minnows. It looks like the state is a paradox, an external enforcer necessary to back up the fragile social super-ego that Freud described in his classic *Civilization and its Discontents*; a necessary evil, a potentially repressive force that we find difficult to live with but, in capitalism's competitive-individualist culture and unstable economy, would probably find more difficult to live without (Žižek, 2010a). On this issue neither conservative statism nor radical-liberal anti-statism has anything to teach us.

When it is not demonizing the state, critical criminology assumes that, in the absence of true transformative politics, reformist social policy can penetrate deeply enough into the core cultural and socio-economic dynamics of capitalism's system. If we had to categorize critical criminology we would have to see it as a slightly more structurally sensitive version of Fabianism, focused on the gradual reform of structural power relations within liberal capitalism's socioeconomic order. How-ever, these social relations, although fundamental to the system, are underpinned by deeper psychosocial forces that liberal-leftist thought has largely been reluctant to investigate. Older leftist schools of thought in philosophy and social science, such as the Frankfurt School's Freudo-Marxism (see Wiggershaus, 2010), which staged a sophisticated and determined effort to reveal these deep psychosocial forces and the elements of the human condition right at the bottom, have been either marginalized or rejected outright.

When critical criminology does approach psychology and subjectivity, it adheres to the principle that pervades critical social science in general, a sort of diluted ideology critique, where ideology is simply viewed as dominant knowledge that can be deconstructed by challenging 'common sense' views. Here, however, this narrow conception suffers from three major problems. First, as we shall see later, there is much more to ideology than mere cognitive knowledge. Second, the term 'common sense' fails to distinguish between (1) the everyday common sense reproduced by the hegemonic culture that operates on behalf of the elite, and (2) the everyday common sense that is the product of both the experience and the parallax view that individuals become privy to by living in neoliberalism's impoverished and abandoned social recesses. Third, not everything that mainstream criminology has constructed is completely wrong. Being a creature of the liberal left, critical criminology should include in its deconstructive remit a reflexive deconstruction of itself, and of course a deconstruction of the intellectual cult of deconstruction, to encourage a programme of theoretical sophistication and improvement. The more intelligent conservatives ask as many searching questions of an outmoded radical criminology as radical liberals ask of an outmoded conservatism.

In recent years strain theory, one of the most enduring yet paradoxically marginalized schools of thought in criminological theory, has been brought closer to the critical criminology camp in order to cut underneath these crude and ailing structural power theories and provide some detail about the localized situations and micro-relations in which individuals get caught up. It has been blended into the work of a number of contemporary theorists. Often viewed as rather traditional and conservative, it has been modified in the critical tradition. Cloward and Ohlin (1960) had modified Merton's (1938) original theory by arguing that positions in the class structure would determine, or at least heavily influence, the individual's likelihood to resort to illegitimate means of achieving legitimate goals. This basic idea lost popularity somewhat in the 1980s, but since the early 1990s it has been revived and further refined in what we might call *contemporary strain theories*. Two contemporary variations from the USA continue to have some impact on criminological thought.

First, Robert Agnew (1992), with his general strain theory, argued that it was not just the broad, structural social relationship between cultural goals and blocked opportunities that created strain, but numerous personal negative situations and relationships in which others block the individual's immediate opportunities – which might not all be economically derived – to satisfy the broad goal of living a fulfilling life. For instance, abuse in the school or family or rejection from a social group might prompt drug use or violence as a means of coping with the strain placed on the individual as specific goals are blocked by specific people in specific situations.

Second, institutional anomie theory argues that the USA's competitive, materialistic cultural drive, which is based in the market economy, has intruded in society's other institutions – family, government, work, welfare, education and so on – to tilt the balance of function towards the economy and reduce the relative power of these institutions and their ability to reproduce the norms that regulate this powerful drive (Messner and Rosenfeld, 1997). This basic theory was incorporated into left realism by Elliott Currie (1997), who took a more radical position and pointed out that the market economy, a uniquely pure and destructive version of which dominates life in the USA, does not just tilt the balance of power away from society's vital institutions but actively corrodes and displaces them. In some places, such as ghettos in deindustrialized areas, it has virtually destroyed them. British theorists such as Simon Hallsworth (2006), and Jock Young (1999) with his notion of 'social bulimia', argue that a more dynamic process comprising cultural inclusion and socioeconomic exclusion working in tension with each other – young people are drawn into consumer culture but simultaneously excluded from lucrative employment and positions of social status – explains why some people will resort to illegitimate means to satisfy desires for consumer objects.

These contemporary theories are very intelligent attempts to revive, modify and enhance the explanatory power of strain theory. However, all classical and contemporary strain theorists, as well as failing to answer the perennial question of why only *some* individuals who experience similar circumstances commit crime, assume that there is something natural about the competitive and materialistic drives – Durkheim's (1961) 'malady of infinite aspiration' – that shape personal desires and goals. Therefore consumer culture is drawing upon a natural, inexhaustible source of energy in human beings, rather like the human psychic equivalent of geothermal or solar energy. Currie (1997) also notes the destructive power of the market and its associated culture, whilst the other theorists assume that the powerful drives and desires for material success, social status and individual freedom behind the American Dream can be regulated by increased opportunities and stronger institutions in a fairer society. This assumes that the problems of inequality, destruction of ways of life and crime can be rectified by piecemeal value-driven cultural and institutional change within the current system of liberal-capitalist democracy as it stands.

Following this reformist principle, Agnew (1992) diversifies and individualizes strain theory by arguing that the various causes of strain can be addressed by corresponding forms of intervention in specific micro-situations. Therefore, logically, these contemporary strain theorists must assume, first, that these drives and desires are not so destructive and toxic that they cannot be tamed. Second, with the exception of Agnew, they must also assume that late-capitalist societies can be reorganized – perhaps by democratic political institutions or by social movements exerting pressure on culture and big business – in some way that will provide everyone with ample opportunities for success, and also repair the social institutions that have been damaged by the disruptive forces of the market. Agnew assumes that diverse desires and blockages have equally diverse sources in plural micro-situations, and therefore tailored interventions can simply carry on indefinitely stamping out myriad little fires as and when they occur.

As we have seen, the assumptions underneath strain theory are highly questionable. To revive the criminological imagination in a relevant form we need, first, to understand that today's consumer desires are not timeless and natural but peculiar to consumer culture, with its ability to manipulate human anxiety and unconscious drives, as it has developed and become central to our lives across the course of modernity and capitalism. Second, we need to imagine an inevitable near future of resource depletion in which these drives and desires do indeed become increasingly toxic, unlimited opportunities for all cannot be provided, institutions cannot be fully repaired and the sources of discontent are not as diverse, situation-specific and manageable as pluralists such as Agnew like to think.

For us, critical criminology must find ways to theorize the paradoxical condition of subjectivity in late modernity. 'The powerless' are certainly victimized actors in the structural sense. However, in the cultural sense many of 'the powerless' seem to be quite driven to escape their condition by adopting some of the exploitative and predatory habits that are reproduced by the system's fundamental exchange logic – get more out than you put in – and practised by the worst examples from 'the powerful', the elite business and political class.

Postmodernist criminology rejected this notion of essentialist subjectivity and, extending the theme of pluralism and diversity, understood diverse cultures as potential sites of 'resistance' to the dominant central power of government, business and mainstream media. It grew out of postmodernism, an intellectual movement that accused Western modernity itself, not simply capitalism, the ruling class or traditional masculinity, of the violent subjugation of marginal populations and alternative ways of life. Modernity's big problem was its Hegelian teleological commitment to progress, universalism and totality; the idea that there is one best way of life, modernity will inevitably lead us all to it and everything else must be cleared out of the way. Thus modernity's culture, governments and systems of control attempted to impose this 'one best way' on all cultural groups, with disastrous results such as Stalin's Gulags, the Holocaust and the insidious systems of surveillance and control that now operate across the industrialized world.

To the orthodox postmodernist, 'crime' is little more than the social construction, exclusion and criminalization of 'otherness', ways of life that do not fit modernity's dominant universal model. We can see how this is diametrically opposed to the zemiological 'harm' perspective, which accepts the truth of universal core harms and criticizes the inability of the law to evaluate harm fairly and apply its power where it should be applied. Deconstructionists, however, argued that we should abandon the notion of universal truth and encourage a variety of arguments against it, thus creating a permanent condition of proliferating difference and change. 'Truth' is just a temporary convention created by language and discourse. If this is so, then 'crimes' are nothing more than temporary 'discursive objects' constructed by the classifying power of modernity's dominant – or 'privileged' – languages and discourses. Postmodernist criminological theorists argued that, to reduce crime, we must decriminalize wherever possible, break up universal morality, devolve culture and encourage legal pluralism. Each cultural group that makes up a plural society must be allowed to set its own social norms and legal rules.

In the 1980s and 1990s, postmodernism generated a good deal of excitement amongst the intellectual community. The importation of postmodernist thinking into criminology seemed to give critical criminology the added breadth, depth and flexibility it required to cope with an increasingly fragmented cultural world. Orthodox postmodernism offered a total critique of the modernist totality, which placed it in the paradoxical position of being a grand narrative against the idea of a grand narrative. However, it could attempt to do so only by descending into 'strong relativism' (see Hall, 2014). Strong relativists argue that there is no universal morality, simply many moral perspectives, and therefore we should be very careful about criminalizing any activity apart from brutal pre-emptive violence. Murder, rape and the various degrees of serious assault should be criminalized, and perhaps serious harm caused to the natural environment, but everything else should be subject to legal pluralism. However, this principle meant that postmodernist criminological research tended to focus on peripheral 'crimes', such as drug-taking, prostitution and anti-social behaviour. It ignored the serious crimes that cause harmful consequences about which there is near-universal agreement. Studies of crime trends show that many harmful crimes such as rape and domestic violence are not 'peripheral' but common, and that many other examples, such as homicide and violent assaults between unrelated adults, rise significantly during times of socioeconomic disruption (Reiner, 2007; Currie, 2009). Postmodernism's strong relativism ended up distracting criminology's attention from what should be its main focus and lowering the discipline's credibility amongst the general public, especially those who had been victims of serious crimes.

Affirmative postmodernist criminology grew out of the recognition that postmodernist criminology's tendency to gloss over 'core consensual' crimes was lowering its credibility. Drawing upon more optimistic affirmative postmodernists who argued that we could distinguish between valid perspectives and those which were simply absurd or destructive (see Henry and Milovanovic, 1996), affirmative postmodernist criminologists argued that cultural groups could be encouraged to produce their own positive self-image by recognizing that not all their transgressions of the law and dominant social norms were harmful. Many transgressions are liberating and life-affirming, and communities can recognize the difference between these and more destructive practices. Communities can be largely self-policing, reducing destructive practices by applying the 'social pressure' exerted by various anti-victimization movements to the perpetrators (see Ericson, 2006), calling upon the criminal justice system only in very rare extreme cases. This seems to suggest at least some elective affinity between affirmative postmodernism, anarchism and, if not libertarianism, what we might call extreme devolved liberalism.

In the practical sense, anyone who has seen a whole community intimidated by one criminal family will know that the affirmative postmodernists are, on one hand, overestimating the community's ability as a courageous and coherent social organizer, and, on the other, forgetting the previous degeneration of some 'communities' into lynch-mobs. In the philosophical sense, by claiming to make the distinction between benign and destructive transgressions, affirmative postmodernism thus abandons relativism and brings back in through the back door a universal conception of good and evil – to be used locally, judiciously and sparingly, but universal nonetheless. We can be largely relativistic, but with universalism and moral absolutism kept in reserve just in case really nasty stuff happens here and there. Therefore this position is no longer 'postmodernist' in any meaningful sense of the word. It is simply democratic liberal pluralism dressed up in new clothes. By retaining the notion of a 'thin core' of universal morality, and therefore acknowledging that some destructive acts should be either normalized or criminalized, affirmative postmodernist criminology also focuses on peripheral activities such as 'edgework' (Lyng, 2005) and graffiti, trying its best to ignore the serious 'core consensual' crimes that, in some places, are harmful and more common than these criminologists like to suggest.

By adopting a post-structuralist approach to language, culture and the order of the social world, which suggests that reality cannot be clearly represented and truth and meaning cannot be firmly established, both forms of postmodernist criminology were rather evasive and ambiguous about the often grim realities created by the shift to neoliberalism and the growing structural inequality and cultural nihilism that can be seen within it. Nihilism is a condition created by the loss of commitment to any sense of good values, and many have argued that it is the unavoidable destination of the relativism that postmodernism advocates and the accompanying displacement of substantive values by the homogenizing exchange-value imposed upon us by capitalism's totalizing marketplace (Whitehead and Crawshaw, 2013). By distracting attention away from the frequent serious harms appearing in the neoliberal world, and by seeking to fragment, localize and reduce political opposition to neoliberalism to multiple cultural 'resistances' that proved to be largely ineffective, postmodernism became a supporter of neoliberalism by default. Obviously, this is not what critical criminology requires.

As postmodernism drifted out of fashion, the notion of 'resistance' was taken up by a new criminological paradigm. Retaining a structural model in the background, cultural criminology emerged and developed in the late 1990s to combine symbolic interactionism and subcultural theory in a revised structural and political context. The intention was to look at the way that individuals struggle to create their own meaning and identity in the cultural and socioeconomic circumstances in which they find themselves. Once again bringing the idealist 'moral economy' principle back into play, many cultural criminologists assumed that young people are for some reason keen to 'resist' the dominant norms and values of the capitalist system, but cultural criminology moves on from classical subcultural theory to look at the relationship between youth culture and mass media. The powerful mass media, operating on behalf of corporate capitalism, define crime and young people in ways that 'label' and blame individuals and working-class cultures for criminality. In this way it draws on some aspects of the 'new criminology' and early critical criminology, specifically symbolic interactionism and labelling theory. Populations are encouraged to consume these meanings, which bolsters the dominant ideology and heavily influences the way they see the world and approach politics. However, ideology is not totally effective because young people, who cultural criminologists assume to be relatively autonomous and not entirely taken in by the dominant ideology, resist these mass-mediated meanings by appropriating and reworking them into their own meanings.

Sometimes, these relatively autonomous meanings are created by young people in intensely emotional collective experiences in subcultural spaces, highly stylized and often motivated by what is seen as a natural inclination to 'edgework' (Lyng, 2005). This means taking risks,

appearing skilful and daring, and transgressing the mundane and rationalized everyday existence of family, school, work, mass media,
consumerism and so on in which young people feel trapped and
undervalued. Today's subcultures are also using the new free media made
available by the development of cyberspace to redefine themselves and
construct their own narratives and visions. In these new narratives,
which come from young people's own perspectives and therefore have
to some extent escaped ideological domination, young people can also
redefine harm and crime in ways that question and defy the corporate mass
media's conventional meanings. In a nutshell, young people are involved
in multiple symbolic struggles against society's powerful elite over the
narratives, values and the meanings of all phenomena including harm,
crime and their own identities and places in the world.

The keel of this position is a combination of hard-line social
constructionism, subcultural theory, and cultural Marxism. It tends to
downplay the reality of the harm that some crime causes and places too
much emphasis on crime as a symbolic transgression of traditional
'authority'. It could be argued that young people involved in the more
harmful forms of crime and delinquency are not transgressing but *con-
forming* to capitalism's disavowed core 'values' and practices, which are
exploitative, acquisitive and socially irresponsible. A cursory look at
Facebook would suggest that cyberspace is a realm in which the
majority of young people, with their often brutally competitive symbolic
interactions, are even further immersed in mass-mediated corporate
culture. Put simply, where they are transgressing anything at all, they
are transgressing the system's norms and rules but not its disavowed
'values' and practices (Hall et al., 2008; Buccellato and Reid, 2014).
There is also too much emphasis on sensual expression when most
'volume crime' is mundane, rational and acquisitive. It assumes that
young people are driven by some sort of natural inclination towards
transgression and proto-politics, which we saw as one of the main flaws
of the old 'new criminology' of the early 1970s (Redhead, 2014).

Cultural criminology is not really criminology, it's the sociology of
peripheral mischievousness, and the distinction it makes between this
and serious crime and harm is often unclear. Therefore it joins the mass
media in blurring distinctions and categories, but from its own
perspective – where the corporate mass media condemn the cultural

criminologists prefer to excuse and celebrate. Neither position is helpful. Cultural criminology's real roots are in liberal 'controlology' (Ditton, 1979) and social reaction theory, liberalism's long-running critique of the criminal justice system and the authoritarian state and conservative moral order of which it is a part. Cultural criminology does little work on harmful crimes such as domestic violence, homicide and violent organized crime, yet it also fails to investigate state and corporate crime, which it leaves to more traditional critical criminologists.

One could even argue that, by suggesting that crime is not such a big problem, cultural criminology unwittingly contributes to the political abandonment of victims of serious crime and harm in impoverished locales and weakens political opposition to the neoliberal economic system that created these locales. Cultural criminology also has a tendency to view youth cultures as progressive and morally superior to the main-stream, whereas in reality they are a mixed bag, and, on the whole, they have had no success whatsoever in improving their lot and now exist in a very precarious socioeconomic position. It also puts a huge burden and expectation on young people; social transformations in the past were carried out by serious, determined and organized adults, not adolescents.

At its worst, cultural criminology is *cultural reductionism*, decontextua-lized from historical, political, economic, geographical contexts, where individuals come to the negotiating table as 'blank slates' rather than with heads full of ideology passed onto them by parents, schools and mass media and affirmed every day in the reality in which they have to live. At its best, however (see Ferrell, 2012; Hayward, 2012a; 2012b), when it is firmly connected to the social structures and historical and economic processes that underlie and set the contexts for cultural forms – such as deindustrialization, neoliberalism and the new precarious-ness of the labour market – it can offer sophisticated and less celebratory accounts of how new cultural meanings and forms of subjectivity and practice emerge in these difficult circumstances (Horsley, 2015).

4

THE RADICAL REALIST RESPONSE

Radical realism has a short, punctuated and rather fragmented history in criminological theory. Gouldner (1973) had criticized the romanticism inherent in North American interactionist and subcultural theories, but from a libertarian/anarchist anti-state perspective that, underneath the structural posturing, could be argued to be even more romantic and idealist. The first signs of radical realist dissent against the idealism of left-liberal criminology came from Elliott Currie (1974) in the USA and Jock Young (1975) in the UK. The fundamental critique was that critical criminology did not take everyday crime seriously enough. This, as we have seen, was first pointed out by the right realists in the 1970s. Unfortunately, at the basic empirical level, they were largely right. The rise in crime rates in the USA and UK from the late 1960s to the mid-1990s was not just a 'social construction' of conservative government and media but an indication that more individuals were becoming involved in burgeoning criminal markets that were to some extent replacing traditional labour markets as the deindustrialization process gathered pace. Rising violence and homicide indicated the waning of the partial social solidarity achieved by twentieth century labour politics and a concomitant rise in victims and harm.

Young began to turn against left idealism as it entered a realm of extreme social constructionism to dismiss most representations of crime and harm as exaggerations designed to create moral panics, manufacture consent and justify the 'law and order society'. The fundamental claim that 'crime' as a signifier has no ontological reality can be accepted with no qualms, but this is hardly a revelation because of course no signifier in itself has any ontological reality. Neither, necessarily, does the 'signified', the thought the signifier triggers in the mind of the receiver. Social science's purpose is to get underneath discourse to produce concepts and signs that are good enough to represent important aspects of the complex and constantly shifting objective reality that underlies the communicative process. Thus it can conceptualize important aspects of what we might call consequential reality as it is constantly reconstructed in a process of change, and theorize the actual – in the sense of 'acting' as a generative combination of abstract ideas, actors and actions operating in the real physical and socioeconomic worlds – forces that drive and shape that change. This is an extremely difficult task, but to shirk it in favour of purist constructivism hammers another nail in the coffin of real politics and the possibility of real transformation.

The term 'crime' is a 'social construct' in that it signifies a transgression of social rules, but the way in which this connects to human experience depends on how well these rules have been constituted for the purposes of representing and preventing real harm done to humans and their environments. Abstract forces and human actions allowed to operate under the authority of these rules have real consequences on individuals and their environments, which all but the most extreme social constructionists would admit, but the point is that some constructed representations and rules are more closely connected to that reality than others. Real objects do exist out there external to and independent to the researcher (Bhaskar, 1997; Sayer, 2000). However, the totality of objects is too complex and relatively inaccessible for either empirical observations or everyday subjective interpretations to represent. It requires hard, systematic thought to reveal tendencies, processes and structures, which was the whole point of having a social science in the first place.

It is important now, as the world changes, to reconnect to philosophy in order to improve these conceptualizations. Without some grasp of the world we live in, human beings exist only as *potential* moral agents, and often as default counterproductive agents unconsciously colluding in a system they do not understand. For instance, the ignorance shown by almost everyone – including sociologists (see Chakrabortty, 2012) – to the complex machinations that brought the financial crisis upon us in 2008 is evidence enough of that.

Some time ago Peter Sedgwick alerted us to the failings of extreme social constructionism and naïve left idealism. He had attended the original National Deviancy Conference in 1968 but later became circumspect about its idealist excesses. Later, in his book *Psycho Politics* (1982), he demolished the ideological attempt headed up by the likes of Goffman, Laing, Szasz and Foucault to pass off mental illness as a mere social construction. Some of the book's more revealing passages stress the point that in the 1960s and 1970s the fledgling liberal left were too naïve and ignorant of political philosophy to realize that Szasz was an extreme right-wing libertarian whose insistence on the reduction of social life to private contracts between individuals was a precursor to neoliberalism. In the 1960s criminology was forced to struggle for identity and direction in a new paradigm set by a new opposition to conservatism and neo-classical liberalism. It was not socialist but an unstable and incoherent mix of right-wing and left-wing libertarianism, a new extreme liberal doctrine, on the run from 'authority', which places the freedom of the individual above all but the most minimal social and legal restraints. The left-wing element, as we now know, was to lose very heavily to the right-wing neoliberal element in the 1980s.

Sedgwick, who had had personal experience of mental illness, revealed it as a torture that had very real deleterious effects on the lives of individual sufferers, a reality hammered home recently in Barbara Taylor's superb book *The Last Asylum* (2014), again based on personal experience. Both writers expressed an appreciation of the progressive turn in Britain's vital state-run mental health services, and Sedgwick revealed that the 'cultural revolution' in the 1960s had, perhaps inadvertently, opened the flood-gates to a powerful current of right-wing libertarianism. Foucault's (2006) ludicrously romantic attempt to pass off mental illness as 'pre-modern unreason' is the opposite of its reality. Psychosis, for instance, whether its roots are in biology, psychodynamic relations or both, is a metaphysically intrusive *excess of reason* that terrorizes a subject who is not lost in unreality but is too finely attuned to reality (Leader, 2012). In a similar vein, Young reminded us that 'the reality of crime in the streets can be the reality of human suffering and personal disaster' (1975: 89). The most common and basic 'personal disaster' was the initial entry of young individuals into criminal markets, which, whether by choice, recruitment and entrapment or sheer desperation, put them at risk of violence and retribution from other players in the market *and* the punitive forces of the criminal justice system. It also further alienated them from other community members, intensifying the process of communal disintegration and social atomization and leading to the late-capitalist culture of hyper-competitive individualism that elsewhere we have called 'the society of enemies' (Hall, 2012d; Winlow and Hall, 2013). The disruption of imperfect but settled and potentially political working-class communities during the recession of the 1970s and the deindustrialization process in the 1980s was having real deleterious effects on the quality of individuals' lives, disproportionately experienced by the former working class (Reiner, 2007; Hall et al., 2008; Currie, 2009).

A year earlier than Young, Currie had made a similar point in a critical review of *The New Criminology*:

> Where traditional criminology regarded deviance as innately pathological, Taylor, Walton and Young regard it as essentially healthy. Neither approach seriously attempts to analyze the sources and consequences and political significance of particular kinds of deviance within the framework of an articulate set of political and moral values.
>
> *(1974: 139)*

The drift of former members of communities into criminal markets added an *internal* agentic cause of disruption and decay to the *external* causes that revolved around rapid socioeconomic change. Some communities in and around the larger metropolitan regions dragged themselves out of this parlous situation, usually with the help of inflows of wage-earners, students and immigrants looking for cheap accommodation, but many others never recovered and still remain as local nodes of various criminal markets with higher than average rates of crime and violence (Dorling, 2004; Parker, 2008). Only a small proportion of those who drifted into criminal markets in the wake of the abandonment of community and the project of political solidarity appear on the statistical records (Hall et al., 2008). Penetrative ethnographic studies, starved of research funding, are few and far between. In some locales, the amount of low-level crime that remains unrecorded by criminal justice agencies or victim surveys, combined with the mutation of crime into new and lucrative markets in cyberspace, casts doubt, as we shall see later, on the whole statistical 'crime decline' narrative (Kotze and Temple, 2014).

After the publication of Young's and Currie's initial doubts, probably the first concerted effort to bring the cold light of day back into critical criminology's idealist perspective – which was in danger of drifting off into space as it began to take its own fundamental fantasy too seriously – was feminism (see Heidensohn, 2012), aided later by the pro-feminism of supportive male theorists. This influential movement grew out of a potent combination of feminist identity politics and the new sub-discipline of victimology (see Goodey, 2005). The principal aim of mainstream feminist criminology was to make the victim more visible and to introduce the fact that known crime and victimization are highly gendered phenomena. Crime is a lived experience that often causes the types of harm that are not merely ideational social constructs but suggest at least a degree of firm ontological existence and ethical consensus. Women suffer harmful violence, intimidation and sexual crime in everyday life, perpetrated mainly by men.

However, most feminists operating in the broad field of critical criminology have adopted a realist, experiential approach only in the sin-gular dimension of violence against women. There are certainly progressive thinkers in this camp, but it still remains somewhat bogged down in an obsolete condemnatory radical feminist approach, which tends to single out men and traditional or 'hegemonic' masculine forms for criminaliza-tion (see Carlen, 1988). This reproduces a type of critical criminology that, as we have seen, is still trapped in crude cultural gender stereotyping and structural conceptions of domination. To suggest that violent and domineering practices are primarily expressions of a traditional mascu-linity that is reproduced by everyday acts of performativity – or 'doing gender' – is simplistic and misleading (Jefferson, 2002; Ray, 2011).

However, the fundamental ontological problem in the broad feminist perspective is the gendered concept of harm itself. Whereas the feminist position initially broke ground to bring the reality of violence and victimization back into criminology, the concept of harm was subsequently expanded beyond its limits as the position developed and established itself. This problem of the inappropriate and often extreme expansion and melding of various categories is part of a broader trend that characterizes the post-political era, discussed in detail by the French theorist Jean Baudrillard (1993). During the feminist heyday, before what some feminists called the 'backlash', such extreme expansion results in definitions of violence such as 'any act that causes the victim to do something she doesn't want to do, prevents her from doing something she wants to, or causes her to be afraid' (Adams, 1988: 191). That category is so broad it could mean anything from being imprisoned and tortured to being refused entry to a nightclub. How we might arrive at rational ontological conceptions of harm will be discussed later. In the face of such extreme and chaotic radical interpretivism and the unrestrained proliferation of increasingly dubious perspectives, rational ontological concepts are of the utmost importance. If, for the foreseeable future, we have to tolerate the established, heavily-funded and therefore publicly persuasive yet potentially misleading method of positivist-empiricism, what precisely we are actually counting and analysing must be connected to reality and the ways in which human beings experience it.

Just to reaffirm the perils of empiricism, the feminist and pro-feminist assumption that violence and harm are typical products of traditional masculine culture or 'masculinity' is based on the sort of statistical illusion that empiricists are very good at presenting to their peers and the public. Only a relatively small percentage of the male population commits serious crime or inflicts non-criminalized harms on others. Therefore, despite the inherent unreliability of statistics, although it looks likely that 80 per cent of crime/harm is committed by men, it is 80 per cent of this small percentage, not 80 per cent of the whole male population. It follows that because the majority of men do not commit crime, crime cannot be an expression of 'traditional' masculinity. Nor can violent crime as a whole simply be an expression of patriarchal dominance, even though in some instances of domestic violence this may be the case. We can all agree that social relations in most of human history have been patriarchal in the sense that women have been subordinated and excluded from positions of executive power, but across the course of modernity in the industrialized West the patriarchal power bloc has presided over huge reductions in homicide and violent crime in all internal territories (Eisner, 2001; Hall, 2012a; 2015a). Something is making violence go up and down, but it is not variations in patriarchal dominance. This is a conundrum that feminist criminology cannot cope with, and thus systematically avoids. We can begin moving towards an explanation, as we shall see later, only by developing an understanding of the *pseudo-pacification process*.

Accordingly, when Messerschmidt (1993) argues the standard line that gender – specifically traditional masculinity – is one of the best pre- dictors of violent crime, this applies only to a small number of crimes and therefore a small number of men relative to the overall male population. This problematizes simplistic structural and cultural theories. It could be countered by arguing that the dark figure of unreported domestic violence is quite probably large and most of it is possibly committed by men, but recent research has suggested that this dark figure probably contains a significant amount of violence inflicted on men by female or gay male partners (ONS, 2014), chiefly because males are less likely to report being the victims of violence (Newburn and Stanko, 1994). Feminist studies also tend to ignore the claim that over 70 per cent of victims of recorded violence are young males and the proportion of male victims in the dark figure could be higher (Hall, 2002). It could be the case that 'doing masculinity' is a more reliable predictor of failing to register as a victim than it is of committing acts of violence. There is also, as some feminist scholars have recognized, a lack of research into crimes and harms committed by women, especially violence, and criminological investigations into the gender split in the business elite, the new 'criminal cloud' of online fraud and other forms of mutating and emergent crime and harm, are in their infancy.

Feminism, like all other standpoint positions, tends to rely on inherently dubious statistics constructed and analysed in partisan ways to support its group interests. For instance, statistics showing that 4.7 million women and 2.7 million men are victims of domestic abuse (ONS, 2014), if we believe they might have some reliability and validity, suggest that feminist- dominated criminological research into domestic violence is far too heavily skewed towards female victims and male perpetrators. On such a shaky empirical footing, feminist criminology has given rise to some weak and unsophisticated theories, as feminist scholars themselves have admitted (see Heidensohn, 2012). Overly focused on sexual crimes and domestic violence, feminist and pro-feminist criminology has little to say about the multitude of other crimes and harms, especially the systemic harms caused by capitalist business practices that affect both genders as victims and benefactors.

Possibly the weakest is Connell's (1995) theory of 'hegemonic masculinity' (see Jefferson, 2002; Hall, 2002; Winlow, 2015). Quite simply, contrary to Connell's fundamental argument, physically violent men do not occupy dominant positions in capitalist socioeconomic and political systems, and the state's organized violence is supported by non-pacifists of all genders across the political spectrum. For instance, Ayelet Shaked, a young female member of the hard-line Jewish Home Party in Israel, speaking publically in the Knesset, recently advocated the slaughter of Palestinian women and their children in order to ensure Israel's security and further expansion into Palestinian land (see Cook, 2014). This is not 'doing gender', and it is not masculinism at work, it is the ugly combination of culturalism and nationalism, which can be bought into, expressed, advocated and practised by individuals of any gender.

However, despite these theoretical weaknesses, feminist criminology was at its best when investigating serious forms of violence and harm, and dragging experiential reality out of the shadows into which it had been cast by left idealism and placing it firmly in the foreground. At a time when crude left idealism was in almost total ascendance, the feminist intervention was still the most potent and useful corrective in critical criminology. At its worst, however – its separatist extreme – it is counterproductive to the extent that it can discredit itself and the criminological discipline in the eyes of all onlookers, not just those from the conservative and neoclassical right. Although feminism had lost its radical appeal by the turn of the millennium and was all too easily assimilated by neoliberalism's competitive individualist culture (see Fraser, 2013), its initial impact on criminology had nevertheless been a game-changer. By emphasizing the important point that some crime is an experience of real harm lived by human beings rather than merely a social construct, feminist criminologists performed the valuable task of returning leftist criminology's consequential object – i.e. the consequences of human action within the current system – to the foreground and giving it some ontological reality. In a nutshell, feminist criminology has been strong on the analysis of consequences but weak in the theorization of causes and conditions. However, it is the valuable move of highlighting the *experiential reality* of harm that needs to be followed up by a revitalized criminological theory based on ultra-realist principles and methods.

The emergence of left realism in Britain in the mid-1980s was a culmination of critical thinking about the inherent flaws of left idealism and other mainstream criminological theories. Currie's and Young's early contributions were seminal, and Ian Taylor (1982; 1999) later rescinded his earlier claim in *The New Criminology* (Taylor et al., 1973) that crime was a proto-political act. Left idealism's most prominent flaw was the neglect of the reality of crime as experienced by victims. However, the emergence of left realism was initially a reaction to the success right-realist criminology achieved in its lobbying of US and UK governments from the 1970s. Right realists had always focused on victims, but it was a superficial populist focus because they completely failed to take into account the crimes of the powerful or analyse the complex probabilistic conditions that underlie trends in crime and harm and bring victims and perpetrators together (Hall and Wilson, 2014). Whilst left realists still acknowledged that the crimes of the powerful were not properly addressed and some aspects of law and criminal justice were biased against the working class, they admitted that most petty crime was *intra-class*. In other words most of it was committed by working-class people against other working-class people.

These were the salutary lessons provided by the victim surveys of the 1980s, starting with the Islington Crime Survey. Even the partial and superficial glimpse of sequences of real events provided by orthodox empiricism revealed the many flaws of a critical criminology dominated by left idealism. This neglect meant that radical criminology's theorization of the crime that lowered the quality of life for ordinary people, and governments' strategies for dealing with it, were weak, overly romantic, outdated and too easily overpowered by right realism. Left realism tried to correct these problems and construct a more realistic theory of crime by looking at victims and the harms they experience in the locales where they live, and analysing them in the 'square of crime', a framework made up of four active relational parts: the victim, the offender, the reaction of the public and the reaction of the state's agencies. The idea was to repair and rationalize fractious relations between the four major players. If these relations could be improved, it may be possible to reduce crime.

In the 1990s this analytical framework did have some influence on Blair's Labour government in the UK and, to a lesser extent, Clinton's Democrat government in the USA. However, the crucial underlying contextual factors of security, decent jobs and housing for all, more fairness and equality, and more cohesive communities – which for early left realists should not be neglected in the way we theorize crime or apply strategies to reduce it – in fact *were* largely neglected. Repairing relations in the square of crime did little to alleviate the underlying economic and cultural conditions that created and normalized these 'problems'. Left realists helped to pull us out of social constructionist inertia and called for positive interventions, but not at the depth required to promote any real change.

Matthews (2014) argues that criminology should build on the gains made by left realism to move on to a genuine critical realism. However, in a surreal topsy-turvy gesture he inverts the real and the ideal. He claims that the call for real depth intervention is a form of 'idealism', by which he seems to mean not philosophical or ethical idealism but something like impossible or dangerous utopianism. He demands that instead we should restrict ourselves to the 'realism' – by which he seems to mean 'pragmatism' – of lobbying for piecemeal policy reforms within the context of the current liberal-parliamentary system, which, as we all know, is dominated by corporate interests. Matthews' argument is therefore resting on two fundamental category errors, which he has made by confusing idealism with utopianism and realism with pragmatism.

Contrary to the pragmatic restrictions Matthews seeks to impose on criminological thought, the fundamental realist question that criminology should ask is this: what type and degree of political intervention is required to create the conditions in which the various harms human beings inflict on one another and their shared social and physical environments would be significantly reduced? The root of true criminological realism is therefore a move away from idealism and epistemology towards firmer ontological conceptions of harms followed by a realistic appraisal, carried out with honesty and integrity, of what must be done to effect a long-term reduction of these harms. Answers to the question of which specific types and combinations of piecemeal administrative reforms and deeper structural and cultural change are likely to reduce harm should not be pre-empted and constrained by the politics – or indeed the fears – of the individuals entrusted with the analysis and theorization of the situation as it stands. Ideally, a value-laden yet thoroughly debated definition of harms and their complex causes should be serviced by a value-free analysis of their possibilities of serious reduction. The depth of the intervention required should not be a pre-emptive issue. As Matthews imposes limits on this crucial realistic appraisal he moves us further away from genuine critical realism and closer to the administrative pragmatism that bogged down left realism in the 1980s.

In fact neither social transformation nor a perceptible amelioration of harms is possible without a realistic appraisal of our current situation and the forces and process that have led to it. Although some individual left realists continued to write with critical depth, as a movement left realism faltered as it mutated into left pragmatism and became intellectually bogged down in its own compromise between critical criminology and administrative criminology. It became progressively more inclined towards its administrative role of providing neoliberal governments with pragmatic alternatives to the popular right-realist strategies of imprisonment and securitization. In the main, most left realists eventually became little more than 'edgy administrators', with a left-pragmatic approach that flattered to deceive, rather than critical realists determined to identify and grapple intellectually with capitalism's structural forces and processes and their very real consequences.

A large injection of critical theory or critical realism could have revived left realism, but it had already established the principle that deep political intervention was impossible (Lea and Young, 1984). Thus it was founded on what we will investigate later as the pragmatic negative ideology of *capitalist realism* (see Fisher, 2009). This ideological turn of late capitalism, which, in an era of triumphant neoliberalism, has convinced the population that no fundamental alternative to capitalism is feasible or desirable, to the extent that even what were once regarded as standard social democratic reforms within the capitalist system – publicly controlled investment, progressive taxation, nationalized major industries, state-run health and secular education, and so on – can be made to appear extreme and unwise (Winlow and Hall, 2013). Sinking rapidly into its own pragmatic quagmire, left realism settled on standard legal definitions of crime, ignored broader harms and contributed little to the philosophical debate on whether legal categories properly represent the harms experienced by ordinary people. It acknowledged underlying contextual problems but had little concrete to say about how to reform them beyond the level of the local community and criminal justice agencies. Major problems, such as unemployment, which need radical structural reform of the economy, were beyond the scope of left realism and criminology in general. Put very simply, pragmatism limits itself to what *can* be done given current structural restraints, whereas true realism tries to understand what *must* be done in order to significantly alter or replace current circumstances and their associated tendencies.

In the 1990s criminological theory took a further pragmatic turn, moving towards the administrative 'crime science' field at the centre of right realism, which was exclusively focused on crime reduction and risk management. Contemporary risk theory began its life in the work of the sociologist Ulrich Beck (1992). Working within the strict confines of the European social democratic mainstream, he argued that in late modernity we human beings were beginning to recognize harms such as ecological degradation and pollution as our own doing. The new cultural awareness of risk was thus prompting us to consider ways of dealing with hazards created by our current way of life, but without significantly changing it at its cultural and economic roots. Beck wrote little about crime, but throughout the 1990s some criminologists and practitioners began to regard crime not as a bad and avoidable thing whose underlying causes and conditions should be reduced by political intervention, but as an inevitable risk to be managed by a combination of public and private agencies. Some radical criminologists pointed out the social inequality of risk taking and the clash between the encouragement of risk and the criminalization and containment of risk (O'Malley, 2010), but, in the main, the field of risk became dominated by administrative criminologists who ignored the more sophisticated sociological studies of 'risk society' to focus on the pragmatic means of containment and crime reduction.

This rather cynical and fatalistic 'risk management' approach played into the hands of the right realists discussed above, and also the administrative criminologists, who welcomed it as a means of gathering more support for crime science and the study of crime-reduction strategies as the only credible form of criminology. We have no axe to grind with administrative criminology as such or its basic function, but we certainly do when it seeks to monopolize the discipline and marginalize politics and critical thought. This certainly seems to be its ambition. It made a decisive comeback from the 1980s onwards, dominating funding streams, changing the nature of criminological research departments in universities and even impacting on promotional patterns. Now, in the big research universities in the USA and the UK, income-generating administrative researchers move rapidly up the ladder to professorial posts. Dissenting intellectuals are becoming a thing of the past (Jacoby, 2007). This leaves us with a rather bizarre situation where the more interesting and theoretically sophisticated criminological thinkers can often be found in universities further down the hierarchy, although this is not a hard and fast rule.

Risk assessment involves categorizing individuals, social/cultural groups and neighbourhoods according to the criminal risk they pose, rather like a motor insurance company assessing risks amongst drivers, and targeting the crime-fighting resources provided by the criminal justice system and the private security industry at the 'riskiest'. Thus crime can be reduced in an efficient way without any political intervention in the underlying conditions – deracinated communities, poverty, inequality, insecurity, consumer culture – that tend to increase it. The adoption of the principle of 'risk management' increased the perceived need for advanced techniques of surveillance, control and incapacitation. This accelerated our decline into a post-political age where we have lost faith in our ability to replace or even significantly improve the underlying conditions in which harmful criminality flourishes. The call for 'efficiency' shifted the balance from public to private security, and narrowed the 'political' argument in criminology to one that simply supported public control – welfare, policing and so on – as it was threatened by the 'commodification' of control by the private sector (Newburn, 2001). The move to 'risk management' heralded a cynical, defeatist post-political era in which the efficient protection of a depoliticized public displaced the traditional ambitions of both reforming offenders *and* transcending the difficult underlying cultural and economic conditions in which they live and drift into criminality.

However, whether it was integrationist or pluralist, conservative or radical, sociologically-based criminology had always experienced great difficulty with the concept of subjectivity. As we shall see in the next chapter, its various schools of thought tended to import off-the-peg philosophical and psychological theories to construct models of subjectivity to suit its preferred political and ethical positions. *Psychosocial criminology* is a contemporary effort to bring psychological and sociological criminology together in a true fusion of psychological and social factors, beyond mere social psychology. The current antipathy between psychology and criminology has a lot to do with criminology's resistance to mainstream psychology's individualized notions of causality. Mainstream psychology has the mirror-image of sociology's problem and a subsequent poor track record in assimilating social, political and economic factors in its theories.

Psychosocial criminology offers the criminological discipline an opportunity to revisit domain assumptions about subjectivity (see Gadd and Jefferson, 2007), many of which are obsolete, and reformulate them in the light of contemporary developments in other disciplines – neuroscience, philosophy, anthropology, economics, politics and so on. For instance, G.H. Mead's (1934) theory of the 'self' as a product of social interaction internalized in a conversation in the individual's psyche is quite probably wrong because it can only account for the malleable 'self-image' – how the subject sees itself through others – but not the original emergence of the subject itself as its unconscious drives and desires, hungry for coherent meaning and partly forged in real experience, seek to escape from the material body to become somehow orientated to various external symbols and meanings (see Johnston, 2008). By revisiting, questioning and reformulating its basic domain assumptions, critical criminology might acquire a firmer grasp on the vital and very difficult issue of subjectivity.

Psychodynamics has made a comeback in psychosocial criminology. Contemporary applications of psychodynamics have so far been very interesting. Adlerian theories focus on the often anti-social ways in which individuals respond to their sense of inferiority or lack of self-esteem, whilst Kleinian theories focus on family dynamics and object relations, or the way that young children build their inner identities in dynamic relations with other family members (see Jones, 2008).

Moving along these paths and others, psychosocial criminology has very good intentions and huge potential in the realist fold, but so far it has resisted extending its analyses beyond the micro-levels of the family, the peer-group and the community. There has been little work on how the broader cultural system intrudes in the family – for instance consumer culture and mass media – and even less on individuals' roles in the ideological and practical reproduction of the socioeconomic system that excludes and oppresses them. Some of the Kleinian (1975) 'object relations' work, in particular, avoids the broad socioeconomic system and seems to be vying for a place in the administrative criminology sector by looking only at dynamic relations between individuals at the micro-level – especially in the family – in which standard social policy and social work interventions can be made.

Psychosocial criminology's potential for producing convincing explanations of criminal and harmful activity is currently on hold. It can be realized only when the sub-discipline equips itself to analyse broader and deeper contexts and all levels of causation from the micro (family and peer-group relations) to the meso (space, local environment and cultural norms) and the macro (structured socioeconomic relations, ideology, economic logic, demographics and geopolitics) (see Hall and Wilson, 2014). However, as we shall see later, Lacanian and Žižekian psychosocial theories, which can be used to deepen and extend the critical realist position, are possibly more useful because they can place the psychological development of the subject in these deeper and broader social contexts.

5

UNTANGLING THE POLITICS OF CRIMINOLOGICAL THEORY

Why have so many competing and often incommensurate criminological theories proliferated over the past 200 years? How do we contextualize and make sense of these complex theoretical developments, and how do we move on? Should we simply carry on empirically testing our theories as they come along? Unfortunately, empiricism is the most ideologically loaded of all our instruments of enquiry. At its best, in a perfect world of pure democracy and transparency, it could alert us to sequences of events that provide fleeting glimpses of possible shifts in the abstract underlying forces and processes that shape our lives. However, at its worst in today's imperfect world of power politics, it is a mercenary pseudo-science that can serve any political group in power or out of power, or indeed any cultural group in civil society with an axe to grind.

'Data' can be produced in quantitative or qualitative forms by empiricists to prove dubious hypotheses and theories about almost anything. Right down to the initial conceptualization of the phenomenon and the dominant research agenda – which of course selects which phenomena are to be funded and researched and which are to be ignored – the empiricist process is heavily ideological. Because of empiricism's credibility and its political versatility – in the sense that populations are by now accustomed to its language of statistical sound-bites and it is willing and able to serve any dominant political group or subdominant cultural group – empiricism is the most efficient, flexible and ubiquitous means of ideological reproduction. For instance, statistics can be used by neoliberal governments to 'prove' that unregulated capitalism produces more equality and less crime, or by radical feminists to 'prove' that one in three women has been the victim of male violence. Alternatively, statistics can be used by socialists to 'prove' that capitalism produces more inequality and more crime, or by conservative women who believe in the hetero-sexual family as an essential social building block to 'prove' that only one in thirty women has been the victim of male violence.

Who is right and who is wrong is not the point and never has been; the point is that statistics and qualitative data can be constructed and presented to the public by whoever has access to the research agenda and the authority, skills and resources to conduct research. Because social research is an expensive business, the credibility of projects and the insti-tutions that conduct them is more often than not determined by their financial turnover expressed as 'income generation and income expen-diture'. The distribution of resources is set by approved dominant and sub-dominant political and cultural agendas, so those groups with authority and influence on either side of the political spectrum get the chance to 'prove' their hypotheses on a scale large enough to achieve some degree of credibility while those who lack authority and influence do not.

Therefore empiricism is a powerful ideological instrument because, in the short run, it can be used to increase the credibility of any interest-group that has the resources to conduct the sort of professional research that can impress the public simply because it is expensive, large-scale, ostensibly rigorous and contains what looks like technical sophistication in its data analysis. Some positivist research projects have produced data and subsequent assertions about rates of crime and causes of crime that are quite simply absurd (Young, 2004). These findings might appeal to the interest-groups who simply seek confirmation of their own world view, but, in the long run, they only serve to discredit criminology in the eyes of the wider public. Put simply, the ability to conduct expensive empirical research is quite often an exercise in ideological confirmation bias.

Thus reality is empirically represented as it unfolds just as history is written when it has unfolded – by the more powerful and influential political and cultural groups who manage to get their preferred issues on the political agenda and their snouts in the trough of the social research industry's resources. If empiricism at its very best can reveal a sprinkling of observable truths as perceived events – if not underlying systemic forces and processes – powerful agenda-setters can too easily distort these truths and explain them away with their overpowering ideological clout. Where truths hit everyday individuals in the face as they experience reality's events as *concrete universals*, those with supercharged empirical power can simply ignore them and go out to prove something else instead. We have to suspect that the powerful elite already know the truth anyway, and therefore 'speaking truth to power' is less useful than one might think (Winlow and Hall, 2013), but they can also use their superior resources to construct pure fictions at the empirical level for public consumption. For instance, the current UK coalition government can statistically 'prove' that unemployment is falling by counting anyone who is on a zero-hours contract or does one hour or more of waged work per week as 'employed'.

It is not that empiricism is intrinsically and irredeemably useless, but simply that on its own, without some revision of the political agenda and revealing theoretical breakthroughs to improve its conceptualization process, it cannot escape from the conditions in which it has been captured and corrupted. It is far more easily deployed in the task of reproducing those conditions than challenging and transforming them. Truths that are uncomfortable to dominant or subdominant social groups can be ignored or invalidated and marginalized by empirical work, eventually to be forgotten until such time that they return in the realm of experiential reality to become symptoms that blight us once again. As Sigmund Freud (1984) once said, what is repressed will always return.

At this point we must make a bold statement about the way the criminological enterprise is run on both sides of the Atlantic. We have to transcend the orthodox notion that theories can be 'empirically tested' in order to prove them true, false or a bit of both. It is impossible to perform true tests of theories, unless theories themselves are confined to localized single issues at the micro-level, in which case theory is the slave of empiricism's limitations. True testing of broader and deeper theories is either too expensive, impractical or politically impossible. On the other hand, extreme social constructionism promotes political inertia by constantly throwing up a smokescreen around reality and dissolving all social scientific endeavours into an interminable language game. This has gone beyond an endless discussion about the meaning of words and concepts to an abject post-structuralist position which tells us that meaning is always slipping and sliding and therefore the connection of our concepts to reality can never really be established, even for a short period of time in the process of 'becoming' in a changing world.

To understand the criminological research agenda, what's on it and how it got where it is, we have to understand the main political and cultural players in the Western world, their underlying ontological ideas and ethical values, and the influence they have exerted on the general social scientific agenda. All the criminological schools of thought outlined in the first three chapters are founded upon underlying complementary ethical and ontological assumptions, which demand that we accept their various beliefs about human nature, morality, freedom, authority, harm and the role of the state in our lives. By 'complementary' we mean that each political paradigm – conservatism, liberalism, socialism, feminism and so on – has adopted specific ethical assumptions about what is good and bad, and ontological assumptions about what does and does not exist in the world, to suit its own world view and its beliefs about what is the best and most feasible way of organizing our socioeconomic lives to ensure our prosperity and security.

Social scientists talk a lot about 'power' and 'the elite'. A perfect pluralist democracy in which all groups have equal representation and equal say would be a fine thing, but it has never existed and it is not likely to exist as long as business interests dominate politics. However, while it is true that powerful elite groups in society have the ability to impose their world views on everyone else and ideologically hoodwink some of the population into accepting their validity by sheer force of repetition, it is not necessarily the case that the world views of the relatively less powerful groups that have managed to lever themselves onto the political and cultural agenda are more truthful and in tune with reality. When we familiarize ourselves with the political/cultural groups outlined below, we might want to take a few minutes to reflect and speculate what life might be like should one of the currently subordinate groups get to run things and acquire the power to define crime and harm and set research and policy agendas. This is not to suggest that the world views of the various groups are entirely invalid. Even the most abstract ideology, as Slavoj Žižek (1989) reminds us, has a small kernel of truth in it.

However, ideological sifting aside, what should be more interesting to social scientists are the experiences and repressed views of what the social theorist Jean Baudrillard (1983) called the 'silent majority', those who have little or no representation on the current political and cultural agendas, or whose experiences are filtered through the more dominant ideological groups and misrepresented in one way or another. This constant multipolar misrepresentation is one of the main reasons why, as we shall argue later, criminology needs a new 'ultra-realist' agenda. We will also see that, paradoxically, although it rejects idealism and interpretivism, ultra-realism is not an attempt to reject ideology and interpretive powers per se in search of pure large-scale empirical truth. As we have seen, the dream of pure empirical truth produced by scientific methods – especially when exclusively positivist methods are used – is multi-purpose ideology in its purest form, an ideological mercenary that can serve any political purpose.

Ultra-realism is an attempt to use a combination of ethnographic methods and sophisticated theory in order to dig underneath existing political positions and their associated ideological assumptions and social scientific paradigms in order to construct *parallax views* (see Žižek, 2006). These are new perspectives from which the world looks different than it does when viewed from the perspectives presented by existing dominant and subdominant ideological positions. We shall explore the principles and practices of *ultra-realism* in more detail later (Chapter 6), but in the meantime we have to know the basics of the existing political positions and social scientific paradigms that dominate criminology. For Thomas Kuhn (1962) a 'paradigm' is a particular school of thought within a scientific discipline with a set of values and ontological and theoretical assumptions that make up its basic framework, within which whatever is being studied is conceptualized and explained. At the deepest level of all social scientific disciplines, including criminology, these assumptions can be seen quite clearly to have been drawn from the various positions that make up the field of Western political philosophy. Each political philosophy has its own particular idea of the ontology (the study of what actually exists in the world) and ethics (the study of whether things are good, bad or in-between) of human nature and social relations. This is not exhaustive and there are many complexities and crossovers, but the basic grid looks like this:

TABLE 5.1 Political philosophy, ontology and ethics

Political-philosophical position	Ontological and ethical conception of human nature
1 Conservative/theocracy/tradition	Free-willed, wicked, in need of discipline and traditional wisdom/bonds
2 Classical liberalism/rationalism	Free-willed, hedonistic, calculative, but capable of benevolence/sentiment
3 Social liberalism/social democracy	Benign, charitable, affable, sociable, creative, needs care to prevent 'damage'
4 Marxism/socialism	Humanist and/or dialectical, responds to contradictions, seeks transformation
5 Radical liberalism/anarchism	Benign, autonomous, flexible and creative, damaged by oppressive authority
6 Postmodernism/post-structuralism	Playful, sceptical, ironic, malleable, largely benign but can be cynical
7 Feminisms	Gendered, domineering traditional masculinity v. benign creative femininity

These ontological and ethical assumptions about human nature provide the basic platforms on which can be built various paradigms that suggest causes of crime and solutions to crime. Old-school conservatives argue that the fundamental cause of crime is society's failure to socialize and discipline innately wicked individuals. The solution to crime and all forms of incivility is to bond the individual to traditional society and its formal and informal institutions – family, church, community, law and so on – in a relationship of mutual respect and conformity. Classical liberals tend to adopt either (1) an idealist, moral constructivist position, which argues that individuals have an innate moral sense and a duty to obey the law, or (2) a utilitarian position, which argues that innately hedonistic and calculative individuals – seeking pleasure but not necessarily wicked – need to confront in their lives a system of choices in which the pain of punishment always outweighs the pleasure and profit to be gained by doing something illegal or immoral. Social liberals argue that to flourish into creative, sociable and law-abiding citizens, individuals need a fair and nurturing society, which can be achieved by reforming social institutions and practices that exist within the current liberal-capitalist framework, although of course many, such as the family, predate it.

Some Marxists, like socialists, have a humanistic conception of human nature; oppressed individuals have a naturalistic urge to seek social justice, which is manifested in class struggle. Others are more dialectical and argue that human beings respond to the contradictions of logic and justice that can be revealed in the social world and seek its transformation, again by means of class struggle, into something more rational and fair. Others combine the two. Radical liberals and anarchists argue that innately benign, autonomous and rational human beings are oppressed and damaged by their experience as subordinates in brutal, punitive, hierarchal systems. Postmodernists propose an extreme version of the principle first put forward by liberal pluralists and anarchists; malleable, sceptical human beings should be able to determine their own ethics and systems of social organization in local and regional groups.

Therefore, for humanist Marxists, radical liberals, anarchists and postmodernists, relatively serious crimes are committed by the state and big business against ordinary citizens, whilst poor people commit relatively petty crimes out of desperation. Feminists, although divided into various sub-groups, all agree that the relationship between men and women throughout history has consistently been patriarchal, in which men have dominated and felt entitled to dominate women and children, often in oppressive and violent ways. If this is true the patriarchal form of masculinity can be put forward as a principal cause of acquisitive, expressive and violent crimes.

The principle we are trying to establish in this chapter is that all the criminological theories we can find in the canon, discussed in Chapters 2 and 3, have their roots in the ontological and ethical cores of various positions of political philosophy, all of which are founded upon specific but dubious and unsophisticated conceptions of human nature. The relationships between various schools of political philosophy and criminological theories are very complex. We have to deal with a tangled web of crossovers and hybrids, but in very rough terms the relationships between general theoretical paradigms (which are also used throughout the social sciences), schools of political philosophy and specific criminological theories are as follows:

TABLE 5.2 The intellectual sources of criminological theories

Theoretical paradigms	Political philosophies (see Table 5.1)	Specific criminological theories
Conservative	1	Conservative/neoclassical control theories, early psychodynamics
Classical liberal	2	Neoclassical control theories, behaviourism, right realism, risk management
Psychoanalytical	1+4	Freudian/Adlerian/Kleinian 'object relations'/ Lacanian theories
Positivist	1+3+7	Linked to and used by most theories, rarely by radical liberalism and postmodernism
Integrationist	3	Durkheimian/Mertonian: social disorganization, anomie, strain, conflict theory
Interpretivist/ pluralist	3+5	Phenomenology, symbolic interactionism, differential association, subculture
Marxist	5	Structuralist/humanist, radical psychoanalytical and cultural Marxism
Critical	3+4+5+7	The 'new criminology', critical criminology, left idealism, early left realism
Feminist/gender	7+various	Radical/liberal/socialist/psychoanalytical/ postmodernist/post-structuralist feminisms
Postmodernist	2+5+6	Post-structuralism/affirmative postmodernism/Foucauldian theory/risk management

These political philosophies, theoretical paradigms and specific criminological theories all have interconnected developmental histories. The following rough timelines do not indicate the birth of theoretical paradigms in general social science but the *approximate point* at which they were integrated into the canon of criminological theory, to be taught in universities in the USA and Europe, applied in research projects and, in some cases, taken seriously by US and European governments. Various theories were adopted in the USA, the UK and Europe at different times – for instance, before the Second World War British criminology was almost entirely classical, positivistic and psychological – but the list below indicates the approximate emergence of each paradigm in the West in general. Each paradigm contains different theories that are developments of fundamental philosophical principles, outlined above and included in this list:

1800	1850	1900	1930	1950	1960	1970	1980	1990	2000	2010

Control Theories (A)..M

Classical Liberalism (A)..M

        Positivism (A)... M

             Psychoanalysis (NA)....................................X   R.........P

             Integrationism (A)..............................X   R.............P/M

             Interpretivism/Pluralism (A)..M

             Marxism/Critical Theory (NA)..........X   R.....P

                Critical Criminology (NA*).......................................P*

                  Feminism/Gender Studies (A)............M**

                     Left Realism (A).........................P

                     Postmodernism (NA***)......P/M

                        Risk (A).....................M

M = currently mainstream in academia

P = currently peripheral in academia

X = became unpopular in academia

R = revived in modified forms in academia

(A) = widely adopted by government social policy research funders

(NA) = not widely adopted by government social policy research funders

* The 'cultural Marxist' element of critical criminology, which includes a critique of racism, and some of critical criminology's offshoots such as green criminology, are mainstream and fundable

** Gender studies includes pro-feminism, queer theory and the critique of homophobia, all mainstream and fundable

*** The exception is Foucauldian theory, still widely used as a theoretical framework in academia and fundable social policy research

FIGURE 5.1 Timelines of criminological paradigms/theories

This is only a very rough sketch. Paradigms do not start and finish abruptly, and there are many hybrids and crossovers. However, it can help us to make sense of the ways in which domain assumptions about human nature, which are based in distinct political philosophies, have been selected and deselected as the West's criminological canon and its governmental research programmes developed over the nineteenth and twentieth centuries. From this rough sketch we can see the basic shape of criminological paradigms and their relationship to academia and government, and make a few preliminary observations:

1 Conservative control theories and classical-liberal 'rational choice' theories have been the mainstays of academic, governmental and criminal justice thinking and practice in the West for over 200 years. Positivist social research, despite positivism's ontological clash with classical liberalism's assumption of free will, can serve both these positions, which it has done for over a hundred years. This ruling triumvirate is still the *dominant force* in elite academic institutions, governments and the research field.

2 The integrationist paradigm did not achieve as much success across the board as the interpretivist/liberal pluralist paradigm. This suggests that Western academia and governments are inclined towards cultural pluralism and are not convinced that societies can be integrated and coherent. The interpretivist/pluralist paradigm, with its fragmented grasp of social inequality and reformist principles – which means that it believes the capitalist socioeconomic system can be made incrementally fairer for all the various cultural groups and individuals in its domain – has been the only serious challenger to the ruling triumvirate. This is the *subdominant force* in elite academic institutions, governments and the research field.

3 Some theories that achieve some credibility in academia for limited periods, such as psychoanalysis, Marxism and critical theory, have achieved little or no credibility in the field of fundable research. It would appear that Western elite culture does not like the ideas of unconscious drives and structural social conflict, and thus it starves their paradigms of funding and credibility. Whether unconscious drives and structural social conflict exist or not, and how much they shape our lives if they do, is of course an entirely different matter.

4 All critical positions have been forced to incorporate some degree of interpretivism and pluralism in order to gain access to the subdominant category and subsequently become academically credible and fundable. The classic examples are (1) the replacement of highly critical Durkheimian 'social disorganization' theory with the more appreciative 'differential association' theory in the Chicago School in

1930s USA, (2) the advent of cultural Marxism in the 1960s with its marginalization of class struggle and its assumption of multiple sites of resistance, and (3) critical criminology's incorporation of symbolic interactionism, social constructionism, linguistic theories and identity politics in the 1970s as it followed the 'new criminology'.

5   Both these major diversions in criminological theory's developmental path marked out a general shift from aetiology, or the study of the causes of criminality, to 'controlology' (Ditton, 1979) or the study of how society defines criminality and how it reacts against it and tries to control it. This is why Foucauldian theory – fundamentally a monochrome analysis of how the state controls the population by means of the classificatory logic of 'biopower' (see Foucault, 1998) – was selected from a diverse cluster of post-structuralist and postmodernist theories and how it flourished in academia and the research field at the expense of more multidimensional theories. For instance, Jean Baudrillard (2007), another postmodernist thinker – although he did not like the label – refuted the idea of 'biopower' and argued that the individual's identity, perceptions and desires are shaped by consumer culture's simulacrum, a system of sign-objects that has replaced reality to become more real than real, or 'hyper-real'. Ideas such as this, combined with other thinking on consumerism, envy and competitive individualism (see Young, 1999; Hallsworth, 2006; Hall et al., 2008; Hayward, 2012a; Smith, 2014), are of much greater use to the investigation of the causes *and* control of crime and harm, because of course a more refined understanding of crime and harm leads to a clearer understanding of how and why the control system was developed. Nevertheless, this general theoretical consumer-centred paradigm was systematically marginalized in the post-war canon of criminological theory.

6   Effectively, this means that criminology virtually gave up researching the causes and conditions that are correlated with criminality. Aetiology was hived off to positivist psychology and traditional psychoanalysis, an administrative research environment that looks at the individual motivations to crime and how to 'treat' them as 'abnormal' psychological conditions – ADHD and so on. Positivist psychologists and traditional 'object relations' psychoanalysts rarely contextualize these conditions in deeper and broader conceptions of culture, economics, politics and social relations.

7 A criminological discipline that is dominated by conservatism and classical liberalism on one side and left-liberal 'controlology' on the other, with pragmatic administrative schools such as positivism and life-course theory floating in-between and taking opportunities when they crop up, will not show much enthusiasm for a deep, con-textualized and coherent investigation of harm, its systemic motivations and its long-term consequences. The first group are happy with current legal definitions of crime that are not too critical of the business class, whilst the second group are worried that expanding our understanding of harm might give the criminal justice system more justifications for intrusive and punitive control practices that threaten individual free-dom. Criminology has boxed itself into a corner where its dominant and subdominant schools of thought are both gravely concerned about the imagined political consequences of investigating the primary objects of enquiry – structural conditions and individual motivations associated with harm and their complex relationships – with too much scrutiny and honesty. No scientific or philosophical discipline can flourish if it suffocates its own curiosity and avoids its primary objects in this way.

8 The general shape of things from the 1970s onwards seems to be a battle between *dominant* right realism and *subdominant* liberal-left idealism. The traditional struggle between conservative idealism, which promoted the idea of a coherent hierarchal society, and socialist realism, which promoted the idea of a coherent egalitarian society, was rejected in favour of a debate between classical liberalism (now manifested in modified form as neoliberalism) and more radical forms of liberalism. In other words, the real struggle between left and right had been truncated and replaced by an institutionalized debate between the right-wing liberalism and left-wing liberalism that occupy the centre-ground. Henry Ford once said that customers can have any colour car they want as long as it's black. Students of criminology can have any political position they want as long as it's liberalism.

David Downes (1988) detected a shift to aetiology alongside social reaction theory in the 1980s, but he seemed to be confusing what he quite rightly wanted to happen with what actually did happen. Until the left realist intervention in the early 1980s, social reaction theories and the move to intersectional power relations – ethnicity, gender, age, sexuality and some concessions still made to class – almost completely dominated the 'critical' wing. They displaced enquiries into aetiology and specific aspects of the hidden economy, whilst the mainstream remained focused on administrative issues that serviced the operation of the criminal justice and welfare systems. The liberal left had outlawed all notions of 'pathology', even those which did not pathologize individuals or cultural groups but identified pathological currents in the capitalist system itself, and insisted on widespread appreciation of all human life and its cultural forms. Unable to think with true analytical freedom, the liberal left became hampered by its habitual error of imagining crime as some sort of misguided opposition to the system in which working-class individuals were compelled to struggle for status and prosperity.

Criminology's main aetiological question of what motivates people to inflict harm on others remained trapped between the narrow parameters of left and right assumptions: respectively, social deprivation and oppression versus the individual's lack of self-control and refusal of social responsibility. In the post-war era many harmful real events and their underlying probabilistic conditions, along with the inquiry into which deep causative factors lie behind both, virtually disappeared from both the mainstream criminological research agenda and the supposedly 'critical' alternative. Systematic child abuse in major British institutions during this period is just coming to light now. The US and UK crime explosions in the 1980s and early 1990s were regarded rather phlegmatically as temporary problems to be solved by either technical crime reduction or light reformist social welfare strategies.

The liberal establishment's refusal to investigate the possibility of pathological currents in capitalism's deep structural logic and mainstream culture was driven by a ubiquitous and irrational fear best described as *political catastrophism* (Hall, 2012a). Put simply, this means the fear that any form of deep political intervention in socioeconomic and cultural life from a socialist or even serious social democratic perspective will inevitably lead to some form of totalitarian government, the extremes of which appeared in the brutal Stalinist regimes that followed the Bolshevik and Maoist revolutions (see Jacoby, 2007; Žižek, 2001). The liberal logic that dictates intellectual life in the West suggests that if the capitalist system cannot be replaced or politically regulated at its core without risking violent social unrest followed by brutal totalitarian government, what's the point of talking about its underlying structures and processes? Thus liberal intellectual life carries a grim health warning: we can investigate capitalism's social problems and their potential light-touch reformist solutions but we cannot investigate its underlying reality in the sense of associating its real harmful consequences with its real internal logic and deep structures, processes and subjectivities (see Horsley, 2013; 2014a; 2014b).

The weakening of the left's resolve as it was compelled to confront the catastrophic mistake of Stalinism opened the door to the return of classical liberalism in its state-assisted form of neoliberalism. We have discussed this trajectory of post-war Western politics in further detail elsewhere (Hall, 2012a; Winlow and Hall, 2012; 2013; Winlow et al., 2015), but the upshot is that the defeat of the left, partially self-inflicted, ushered in the era of *capitalist realism* and *post-politics*. Very few individuals now believe that an alternative system is possible, therefore traditional oppositional politics has disappeared to be replaced by arguments about how to construct more just and equal social relations within the system as it stands. Social relations tend to be conceptualized in intersectional terms of identity, usually race, ethnicity, age and gender. Where class is included it tends to be expressed in terms of a stratified yet potentially fluid and porous system whose means of ascent can be made more meritocratic, rather than an antagonistic structural relation to be abolished.

In this post-war transition from traditional antagonistic class politics to the politics of identity and meritocracy, the role of social scientists and politicians has not simply shifted from legislators to interpreters (Bauman, 1989) but to highly restrained single-issue interpreters working on behalf of social micro-technicians. Where social scientific theory and philosophy thrived in the era of politics and legislation, and ethnography and theory thrived in the era of interpretation, both have been marginalized in the era of *biopolitics* – here we use Žižek's (2005) precise definition of the management of politically inert bodies rather than Foucault's (2008) woolly notion of general 'global control' over the body – whose main task is to cushion the harmful effects of neoliberal economics and culture on the system's many victims. Social micro-technicians are not really interested in the underlying conditions and causes of harms, only in the individualized and localized nature and diversity of harms, how they impact on victims, how they can be reduced and how victims can be rescued or made more resilient.

The emergence of the social micro-technician in the wreckage of left-wing politics means that there are two main suspects in the murder of ethnography and depth theory in criminology. The conservative/ classical-liberal alliance (henceforth CCLA) is the dominant power bloc that controls economy and culture according to the logic of neoliberal capitalism. The liberal-progressive social administration (henceforth LPSA) is the subdominant and rather beleaguered power bloc in charge of the biopolitics regime, tasked to beg for funds from tax revenues, clear up the mess, lobby for minimal negative human rights on behalf of individuals and intersectional identity groups and propagate the myth that fairness can be achieved within the current system without too much political intervention in core socioeconomic structures and processes. This polite animosity between the dominant and subdominant power blocs has replaced class struggle. What we need to bear in mind for the following discussion is that neither position is a genuine political movement working against the unfair and destructive capitalist system but a *moral enterprise* working within the system and opposing the other one only about administrative matters across a severely truncated middle-ground.

Ideally, the university is supposed to be a crucible of intellectual analysis and debate providing an independent alternative to these two power blocs (Carlen, 2012). However, higher education in the UK and the USA is now mass education, so overloaded that neither beleaguered lecturers nor students have the time to investigate the philosophy and politics that underlie their disciplines' objects of study in any great depth – at least not without burning copious amounts of midnight oil (Hall and Winlow, 2012). Instead, they study the *selected consequences* of their discipline's object of study and how to administrate them. Thus criminologists don't really study the deep causes of crime and harm, only manifest symptoms, victims and social reactions. Only the privileged Ivy League or Russell Group academics can carve out the significant chunks of time required, but most of these privileged academics are conformists who support one side or the other of the dual CCLA/LPSA entity and spend a significant proportion of their time applying for funding to investigate issues imposed on them – 'research themes' – by governments and unelected academic quangos such as the UK's Academy of Social

Sciences. Dissenters tend to attract the pejorative label 'fringe', allowed to speak but neither celebrated nor funded because their wacky ideas defy the 'weight of scholarly opinion'.

Thus students and the public do not get the best theories capable of explaining the world as it is at the greatest possible breadth and depth. Instead, they get what harried researchers can produce in response to the agenda items imposed upon them by governments, quangos and private charities, which together hold the purse-strings. All theoretical perspectives must fall within the parameters set at both ends by the CCLA and the LPSA, with the technical strategies of the criminal justice professionals – situational crime prevention, experimental criminology, restorative justice and so on – trying to occupy neutral ground as they sell themselves like taxi-cabs for hire to incumbent neoliberal political parties. There is no blue-sky thinking in the liberal-postmodern university. In fact there is no blue sky, only the grey clouds of neoliberal economics and biopolitics.

Now that traditional conservatism and socialism are virtually dead, the principal values controlling the criminological discipline are essentially right and left variations of liberalism. On the right, neoliberalism, a modern state-aided variant of eighteenth-century classical liberalism, insists on free markets, punitive and militarized states, personal responsibility for actions, individual reasons for committing crime and efficient means of controlling and deterring offenders. Human beings are free but naturally competitive and hedonistic. These drives can be harnessed to the economy and make us all richer. However, they need to be stimulated yet kept in check by means of cultural and legal rules, both of which should be enforced by punishment. Traditional conservatism plays a far smaller role than it once did in today's politics, but in the CCLA its vestige survives under duress as a junior partner to add a moral dimension to neoliberalism, arguing that faulty socialization and subterranean anti-social cultural values are the main contexts in which individuals become criminal. Most right-wing criminology – sometimes called neoclassical or right-realist criminology – is an imbalanced hybrid of these two basic positions, but dominated by neoliberalism.

On the left, the two main positions are left-liberal and social democratic. The first position emphasizes human freedom and argues that the repression of the state and the conservative collective in an unequal social structure is the main reason for crime; poor people commit minor crimes out of desperation and heavy-handed criminal justice, as well as being unfair, makes things worse by labelling and 'othering' poor people, further alienating them from society. The second position agrees with these basic premises, but sees a greater role for the state in regulating and hopefully reforming the unstable capitalist economic system, using the LPSA apparatus to cushion neoliberalism's blows and thus reduce the primary reasons for acquisitive crime and punitive social reaction. Most left-liberal criminology is a hybrid of these two basic positions.

So far we can see that Western criminology is essentially a two-dimensional 'dual mainstream' discipline consisting of a dominant conservative/classical-liberal paradigm that exists in undialectical tension with a diluted subdominant liberal-left paradigm that likes to call itself 'critical' and 'emancipatory'. Both are essentialist – although the latter exerts huge effort in denying this – and resolutely undialectical. The former posits a wicked/hedonistic human nature whilst the latter posits a creative, benign yet indeterminate human nature. The former seeks to bolster traditional informal and formal institutions of discipline and socialization whilst the latter seeks to liberate the creative individual by dismantling oppressive institutions and unequal, domineering social relations.

Critical criminology is embedded firmly in the latter paradigm. What these paradigms have in common is that they both argue that their respective ambitions can be fulfilled in the liberal-capitalist system as it stands, without disturbing deep socioeconomic structures, cultural values and historical processes, or the fundamental exchange relation that seeks to create a surplus out of each economic transaction. The salient point to draw out of this classificatory exercise is this: all theories that posit the human being as ultimately flexible across the spectrum of good and evil, posit unconscious drives as the main motivating factor in human behaviour, and suggest that the deep transformation of existing political ideologies, socioeconomic arrangements and cultural values is the only way to reduce significantly the human propensity to harm individuals and their environments, experience extreme difficulty in being accepted in the dual mainstream.

Neither of these two polarized meta-paradigms is driven by curiosity and scientific or philosophical enquiry. Conservative criminology outlaws direct criticism of society's core institutions and values whilst left-liberal 'critical' criminology outlaws direct criticism of the role that everyday people play in reproducing the system some of them appear to dislike. What really drives these meta-paradigms and all their associated criminological theories at the deepest level, even the ones that regard themselves as administrative and pragmatic, can be boiled down to two irrational fears: the fear of order and the fear of disorder (see Hall, 2012a). Left-liberals tend to fear order as inevitably oppressive whilst conservatives tend to fear disorder as inevitably chaotic and violent. The criminological paradigms and theories that stir up both of these fears are the ones that have been systematically marginalized. The need to understand the reality beneath these two mystifying and obsolete mainstream discourses, which were produced and continue to be institutionally maintained by their respective fears, is behind the need for *ultra-realism*.

However, at the moment a sweeping move to ultra-realism is unlikely because criminology is under immense pressure from outside. There is a constant influx of outside values and agendas, which is leading to the erosion of academic autonomy. Governments and research councils have various policy agendas, which researchers are paid to evaluate. Thus we have policy-driven research rather than research-driven policy. The very idea of having theory-driven research and theory-driven policy, where academics produce ideas relevant to our current real situation and create research agendas and suggestions for policy institutions to fund, is out of the question. This must be done independently, but academics are under huge pressure to teach orthodox ideas and acquire research funding in the new marketized university.

The historical roots of social research funding in the UK, beginning in the late nineteenth century, are firmly implanted in light-touch Fabian reformism (see Bushaway, 2003). Early social scientific studies were funded by wealthy 'philanthropic' industrialists such as Rowntree and Lever. The political ideologies of 'wet conservatism' and 'social liberalism' still control the research infrastructure, from top research universities and research councils to private trusts. The USA's Social Sciences Research Council, established in 1923 and reliant on private funding from foundations associated with monopoly capitalists such as Ford, Carnegie and Rockefeller, restricted its research to problem-solving and disseminating 'disinterested knowledge' to policymakers. The fundamental principle underneath all funded social research is that liberal-capitalist economies and societies are fundamentally sound. They admit they are not perfect and have problems, but all problems, even persistent social inequality, crime, corruption and environmental degradation, are temporary anomalies and malfunctions that can be solved by government policies, social interventions, technology and enlightened changes in business practices.

Therefore even the most serious problems must never be expressed as the inevitable outcomes of the deep psychosocial, cultural and economic logics, processes and forces that structure and drive forward the capitalist system. To suggest this would be to reduce one's chances of research funding, credibility and rapid promotion in the university hierarchy. In the USA, politicians such Tom Coburn and Peter Wood have recently advocated the reduction of the social, behavioural and economic sciences to that which represents national and economic security (Zaino, 2013). This would fundamentally change the agenda of the dominant CCLA and the dynamic tension between the CCLA and LPSA. Most importantly, it would fully institutionalize what DeKeseredy and Schwartz (2013) have called the 'progressive retreatism' that is currently afflicting social democratic politics, thus far the only effective means of regulating capitalism and cushioning its blows. Social democracy, the only genuinely interventionist wing of the post-war politics, is in danger of receding into history (Reiner, 2012). In today's ideological climate even this reformist movement, once criticized by the left for its compromise with capital, appears to today's pragmatic liberal mind to be wildly utopian because it suggests reforms that go too deep (Winlow and Hall, 2013). Academics need to monitor these developments in the coming years.

So far we can see that in today's stultifying, truncated intellectual climate Anglo-American criminology is divided into numerous theoretical schools, none of which are really going anywhere. What we get is the proliferation of fallacies and superficial truisms, rather than genuine attempts to synthesize ideas that can be put to work. These fallacious discourses have become institutionalized, with societies, panels, foundations, prizes and so on set up to reproduce them into the future. What is lost in all this negative-defensive activity is of course the spirit and practise of open scientific and philosophical enquiry.

The situation is not helped by the way social scientific disciplines run themselves. Social science is not a democracy. Theory has been demoted to the bottom of the pile (DeKeseredy, 2012) to be starved of research funding. Sophisticated theoretical works have even been left out of UK REF (Research Excellence Framework) submissions in favour of bland microscopic empirical studies with immediate 'policy impact'. Social scientists talk of 'theory construction' rather than theory, which means painstakingly building theoretical frameworks like temporary Lego models to suit specific issue-based research projects, and constantly referring to empirical work rather than seeking new philosophical principles for more revealing research and richer explanations. Even if the need for synthesis were to be accepted, some positions, such as Lacanian psychoanalysis and Marxism, have been largely rejected and thus their insights would play negligible roles in any new project of enquiry.

Policy research is not entirely atheoretical, but the orthodox dualistic politics of the CCLA/LPSA entity that governs both public and private funding in the social scientific establishments in Britain, Europe and the USA is very selective about the safe reform-orientated theories – structuration, risk, liberal feminism, post-structuralism and so on – that are acceptable. Money will be splashed out to prove politically approved theories whilst radical or critical theories are starved of the funding required for large-scale empirical testing and theory construction. If we look at the theories in the previous two chapters we can chart their ebb and flow as the politics of the twentieth century changed, and the parameters in which they were forced to work were progressively narrowed. This had the effect of profoundly truncating and domesticating criminological thought of both the right and the left and box-pressing it into an extremely narrow centre-ground.

We are not suggesting that there's anything wrong with social democratic reforms such as job creation, healthcare, anti-violence legislation and so on, or indeed with the moves towards the equalization of social power relations. What we are suggesting, however, is that an open debate on *precisely how deep* these reforms must go – and which other *more fundamental reforms* might be required to have any significant and durable effects on criminality, harm and securitization in our currently divisive and unequal societies – should be at the centre of social science. We will look at what might exist underneath capitalism's social world and its power relations later when we investigate the transcendental materialist *fourth layer* of social reality and how it might be brought into clearer relief by developing the ultra-realist theory we propose.

To do this, theoretical criminology will have to make a quantum leap and look at the social world and its events, values, norms and power relations as *effects*, not causes, of far deeper and very complex causal processes organized by the *fundamental fantasy* and the *fundamental logic* that drive and organize the interactions between the psyche and the socioeconomic and cultural systems. At the moment the hierarchal and ideologically hamstrung institutions of liberal-left sociology and criminology are limited to the study of these *effects* or *symptoms* as causes rather than indicators of what might lie beneath them. Neither faction of liberalism seems to be prepared to invoke the spirit of free enquiry and get down to an ideologically unhindered scientific and philosophical investigation of deeper causal processes and structures. For us, the only way to transcend this impasse held in place by dualistic intellectual repression is to revive the faltering yet still potentially potent realist project (see DeKeseredy and Schwartz, 2013) and move it forward into a new and hopefully revealing ultra-realist phase.

6

ULTRA-REALIST
CRIMINOLOGICAL THEORY

The legacies of left realism, feminism and victimology provide critical criminology with a platform from which, if it can gather its will, it can launch itself forward. Prominent amongst these legacies is the injunction to treat harmful forms of crime seriously and investigate with methodological and theoretical rigour their consequential realities as they are experienced by individual victims and impact negatively on social, cultural and physical environments. Prior to social scientific investigation, a serious philosophical debate is needed on the ontology of harm in order to distinguish between core and peripheral harms (see Yar, 2012; Hall, 2012a). 'Crime' is of course a nebulous socio-legal construction, but we should not assume that harm is too. However, the debate on harm is complex, because, despite having one foot in reality, it can cover a huge range of consequences on a spectrum from an individual's minor emotional upset to the destruction of a whole natural environment.

We cannot provide a typology in this short book, but we suggest that criminology should open up and prioritize a permanent research focus and debate on the experiential reality, ontology and conceptual definitions of harm with a view to establishing and constantly but carefully revising a core set of harms that should constitute the discipline's major foci in the future. Criminological debate should include but also transcend current legal definitions of 'crime', and, without assuming that all current legal definitions have no relation to real harm, investigate the fundamental question of where there might be consensual agreement on what is really harmful and how that informs processes of criminalization and decriminalization.

We must escape the ontological reversal of *multipolar pragmatism*, where definitions of harm are constructed according to the limits imposed on them by the solutions approved by liberal-democratic states or social movements concerned with single issues. This reversal does not open up debate but makes the situation worse by diffusing the principle of theoretical isolationism everywhere. Problems are currently defined by the approved institutional solutions to isolated issues, and the gathering of evidence is thus driven by existing policies associated with these institutions. Ideally, this relation should be reversed: research and theory first, solutions debated later. We desperately need honest, open and free philosophical debate and social scientific research programmes focused on the most pressing zemiological issues, which can inform solutions and, more importantly, indicate the depth and scope of political interventions needed to provide those solutions.

To initiate this debate, criminology should be at the forefront of a concerted attempt to construct a flexible metaphysical field that can in turn be broken down into precise zemiological categories. How might we do this? Yar (2012) argues that manifold social harms are the products of patterns of social inequality. Although he is right that the two are associated, his formulation is the reverse of the social process that structures and reproduces capitalism. In a system based on a culture of competitive individualism and an economic exchange relation designed to exploit and extract surplus from others and the shared environment, the pattern of social inequality based on success in profitable business is the product of the logical imperative *and* the subjective willingness to inflict various forms and degrees of harm on individuals and the physical, cultural and social worlds in which they live (Hall, 2012a). In other words, social inequality is one of the products of the willingness to inflict harms on others.

Where Yar is unerringly right, though, is that an ontologically grounded conception of harm can be based initially on an understanding of social recognition. The denial of basic love, rights, esteem and material survival above subsistence level is indisputable (see also Honneth, 1996). But we must debate the goal of social recognition. In the liberal imagination it is simply the 'avoidance of mistreatment' or the 'preservation of persons': essentially *negative* rights. This must be extended to the *positive* rights associated with human flourishing.

However, neither set of rights can be assured and developed in a world that has transcended the Hegelian Master–Slave relation to reach an even purer relation of unconditional subjugation. In all past epochs the master needed the slave and the slave's approval, no matter how begrudged. Today, in neoliberalism's global hi-tech and migratory economy, capital no longer needs labour in the mass ranks and the settled communities it once did. Labour has only a tenuous bargaining position from which it can seek approval and demand rights. For poorly skilled and vulnerable wage-dependent individuals the bargaining position is virtually non-existent and constant appeals must be made to charity, or whatever *post hoc* forms of benevolentism and sentimentalism the rich and their political servants are willing to fund. Human nurturing and flourishing are low on the agenda for all those who find success in the market difficult.

The motivation for harm exists in *negative* and *positive* forms. The negative form is the space created by the separation of the relatively rich and successful from the precariat, in which multiple harms can be inflicted – sometimes unintentionally out of pure ignorance of their consequences – on the latter and their social and physical environments with relative impunity. The positive form is *special liberty*, the dark side of liberal individualism, a sociopathic anti-ethos that consists of a sense of entitlement felt by an individual who will risk harm to others in order to further his own instrumental or expressive interests (see Hall, 2012a). This has its roots in the logical necessity of business and profit-making at all costs and the urge to exploit and cause the downfall of others in order to achieve positions of security and status in a pan-competitive environment. In a system where the highest status is achieved by success in markets the two forms of liberty are closely interlinked, but often presented as distinct in liberal criminology.

Over the past thirty years or so left realism's disinclination to construct a universal notion of harm at the centre of its discourse and the continued reliance on legal definitions of 'crime' contributed to its decline. It had conformed too closely to liberalism's general inclination to play down harm in order to prevent social overreaction, and – if the majority of harms were ever to be understood by the majority of the population as manifestations of structural relations, corruption and a culture fuelled by obscene drives – the return of politics and possible social conflict. Feminism had entered the fray by insisting that we recognize and act against the serious and harmful consequences of crimes against women, but by the late 1980s the movement had been absorbed into neoliberal culture and politics (Fraser, 2013).

Between 1956 and 1991 the degeneracy and eventual collapse of state socialism and communism allowed liberal and libertarian interest-groups of various types to discredit the once dangerous class struggle, infiltrate the left and quickly colonize it. Various positions within the constellation of postmodern multicultural identity politics now vie for economic success, power and influence in the general capitalist market-place and its attendant institutions. At the same time, the representatives of each position lobby for tolerance to be shown by their competitors. Multicultural identity politics became not a dynamic social transformer but a static umpire, a means of organizing and legislating for people to play hard but fair in neoliberalism's new global economy. Liberals had managed to once more turn social struggle back into what they will always prefer; an atomized pseudo-pacified game whose *doxic* normalization and constant understatement nicely underplays the gravity of the stakes for which everyone has to play: no less than the individual's economic livelihood inextricably linked through market performance to social status and security. Caught up in this political shift, criminology's systematic liberalization, fragmentation and theoretical shutdown caused it to lose sight of the fundamental socioeconomic and cultural contexts in which crimes and harms occur in their various patterns.

An ultra-realist position would demand that this theoretical shutdown should be rescinded and the analytical machinery restarted in a mode of searching realist depth critique that we might call *ultra-realism*. At this point we need to be clear about what we mean by realism and ultra-realism. First of all, there are various types of 'technical realism' we need to avoid and supersede. We have already seen the multiple problems that afflict positivism and empiricism. They are trapped in a realm of superficiality, eternally restricted to observable phenomena, which, because crime and harm are obviously practices that people usually try to conceal, restricts representations of reality more than in any other social scientific discipline. Positivist-empiricist criminology is a generalized *synecdoche*, a Greek word that, literally translated, means a part that always promises to bring to you more of the whole than it ever can. As such, it discourages theorization of depth structures and generative processes, what we will come to know soon as the *intransitive* domain. Nor can it provide us with a sense of ethics or agency, or, unless prohibitively expensive longitudinal studies are conducted on a large scale, with a sense of transformation, the constant 'becoming' that drives our world forward. Nor can it provide us with a sense of *absence*, which, as we will see soon, is also causative at the deep level. Positivist-empiricism is a major component in the representational machine that fetishistically disavows hidden truths by constantly shoving in our line of vision an impoverished, partially-revealed reality constructed by political interests and incurably limited research methods.

However, realism in general has a rather bad name. One reason behind this is that popular culture, politics, philosophy and social science have all been characterized by varieties of cynical realism. These positions essentialize the very worst human propensities and look remarkably like they were specifically concocted to support the political positions of conservatism and classical liberalism and make root and branch socio-economic transformation look well-nigh impossible. Transhistorical conservative realism, as we saw in Chapter 5, bases its ontological conception of human nature on the biblical 'legend of the Fall' from God's grace. In conservative thought, a rigid, pessimistic Old Testament view of the human being as an inherently wicked sinner is often combined with a pseudo-scientific ethological view of the human being as the 'killer ape' (Dart, 1953). The timeless sinner driven by the violent *animus* of Cain is in need of constant discipline and punishment by the cultural forces of tradition aided by the rational forces of modernity. Most control theories, as we have seen, are grounded in this mythical view of human nature. Classical liberalism and neoclassical right realism are based on a similar but more rationalized psychological conception of the human being as a selfish, hedonistic rational calculator, always seeking pleasure and profit whilst avoiding pain and sacrifice. This modernist type of wickedness must be controlled first and foremost by the deterrent effect of rational and proportional systems of justice and punishment.

However, the postmodern era has its own versions of cynical realism. *Depressive realism* pervades popular culture in art, cinema, literature and music, and in many forms of youth culture on the 'street' (Jeffery, 2011). The core of this culture is post-political, cynical and nihilistic, born in the era of *capitalist realism* where all alternatives to the capitalist system seem to have failed, and individuals envisage no change in their lifetimes, just a series of presents – endless, monotonous and in slow decay. There are no heroes, no visions of a better world and no great political projects to transform a capitalist socioeconomic system in which the security of the individual is becoming ever more precarious. Depressive realism feeds us apolitical tales of late-modern selfishness, nihilism, degeneracy and dystopia, the sheer pointlessness and weariness of being at the end of history. Well-known examples include the works of French novelist Michel Houellebecq and the American novelist Bret Easton Ellis (see Jeffery, ibid.). These works and others like them are richly descriptive, sometimes amusing and inevitably depressing, but the important point for our purposes here is that this is a 'thick descriptive' realism that serves no ethical or political purpose. It is as pointless and cynical as the characters and lives it describes; an anti-quality that, ironically, is part of its realistic appeal in today's post-political era. Perhaps its sole potential purpose is the political reaction that might be fuelled by the disgust that can be invoked by the normalized degeneracy it portrays, but it is difficult to tell from which point on the political spectrum such a reaction might be forthcoming.

Opposed to the edifice of conservative and postmodernist cynicism is the rather ailing *left idealism* of the 1960s-vintage 'new left', the radical left–liberalism that still dominates social science education as if it were still new and relevant to today's world. Left idealism was Young's (1975) term for the ideas that influenced sociology and criminology in this period, but it is something of a misnomer. It does indeed see the social world as a configuration of interacting signs and symbols. However, as we saw in the chart in Chapter 5, underneath this discourse, very deep down, lies a disavowed, *naturalistic realism*, the naïve ontological assumption of natural ethical realism, a timeless human orientation to creativity, transgression and struggle for social justice. This is simply the mirror image of naïve right realism's ontological assumptions of hedonism, selfishness and wickedness, the opposing view that can be allowed into liberalism's intellectual clearing house for the sake of balance and the perpetuation of eternal hope amidst permanent political inaction. However, the sheer diversity of human emotion and action throughout history, ranging from extreme genocidal violence to the most uplifting acts of altruism, compels us to understand that human beings, their drives and their desires are more malleable and indeterminate, and perhaps more dependent on circumstances and experiences, than either the right or the liberal-left suggest.

Lying beyond the naïveties that mark the right and left boundaries of liberal thought is the philosophical and social scientific position of *critical realism*. Most critical realists claim that some measured empirical observation is useful, as is the acknowledgement of human meaning and the causal power of agency, but there is much more to social life and its dynamic forces. Roy Bhaskar (1997), one of the architects of critical realism, argued that positivism–empiricism simply reveals the regular recurrence of events but not the structures, powers, forces and processes that make events occur in the way they do. Societies' deep dynamics are not necessarily revealed and 'represented' by empirically observable events; as we have seen, the synecdochal representation of events can throw us off the track more than having no 'evidence' at all.

This is especially true in criminology, where events are often systematically concealed by perpetrators and victims alike and incompleteness is the normal order of things. Empirical research is always preceded by the construction of concepts and hypotheses – nobody gets money to go out on a hunch and have a look around these days – that predetermine roughly what researchers will find. Perhaps, because most corpses are found and means of death established with reasonable accuracy, homicide statistics have a modicum of validity and reliability (Hall and McLean, 2009), but beyond this nothing else does. Movements in the regularity of easily definable, readily observable and less contentious phenomena such as hospital admissions can give sociologists some inkling that there has been some change in underlying causative structures and processes, but 'crime' fulfils none of these criteria. It is a complex social construction, largely concealed and born of contention.

Critical realists argue that empiricism might be useful in conceptualizing what we mean by 'crime', but it cannot help us to reveal the powers and forces, and indeed their very real consequences, that exist independently of our knowledge and existing theories. This is what our theories should be trying to understand, otherwise they will remain, as with conventionalism, eternally wrapped up in analyses of their own internal construction of meanings, or, as with positivism, descriptive and correlational. Positivism can identify causes, but only small disembedded situation-specific ones in the mid-range (or meso level), usually after years or even decades of hypothesis-testing. Both positivism and conventionalism can be seen as ways of deliberately avoiding any contact with underlying structures, powers, forces and processes.

For critical realists, the fundamental theoretical problem in social science is that we must retain the ontological distinctiveness of the individual and the social whole whilst we work out how they necessarily – 'necessarily' because one can't exist without the other – relate to each other. As a way forward, critical realists propose ontological realism in the intransitive realm of 'thing-like' structures, processes, powers and forces that exist independently of our current knowledge of them, combined with a qualified and partial epistemological relativism in the *transitive* realm of things that are the products of our knowledge and activity. If we ignore the distinction and the relationship between the intransitive and transitive realms we ignore the constraints that reality places on our knowledge and activity.

There is, critical realists argue, a thing-like quality to structures, relations, forces and mechanisms in the intransitive realm. There are no universal laws, but under certain conditions there are *probabilistic tendencies*. Even some measured and careful prediction of tendencies is possible. For instance, rapid industrialization or deindustrialization, because in their different ways they both disrupt established means of livelihood, will tend to increase crime, harm and social unrest; in fact we could see abrupt loss of livelihood on a mass scale as a major form of harm in itself. Securitization and incarceration will tend to reduce some crimes, if not in an ethical or progressive manner because of course their repressive practices are also major forms of harm, but, yet again, this is to some extent predictable. Of course these thing-like powers and effects are mediated by human beings and their ability to construct meaning and act as moral agents in the world, but to suggest that their thoughts and actions are not in some way restrained and influenced by their existence in the intransitive realm of the 'real' would be excessively naïve.

When we speak of human beings and their relations to ideas and structures, the term 'influence', because it incorporates notions of agency and indeterminacy alongside tendency, is more precise than the more mechanistic 'cause'. However, influence is still a potent force. In some circumstances, especially those where mass-mediated ideology operates efficiently and alternative actions in the real world are made very difficult by repression and the repercussions of systemic logic – for instance, a wage-dependent individual involved in a long-term strike or protest will risk state violence, loss of income, inability to pay debt and bankruptcy – it can be so strong that it acts very much like a 'cause'.

Critical realism focuses on agency, structure and causation in a changing world. We do not 'create' social structures in the sense of original genesis, but we reproduce them and have the potential to transform them. However, as we act within them, they feed back on us and causally affect and influence what we do. Structure is more than an ideational 'concept', therefore we must move beyond social constructionism and postmodernism. Such constructivist positions don't deny that extra-discursive things exist, just that we can't know much about them as things-in-themselves; anyway, they can't determine what we think or do and we can transform them by changing meaning and acting differently. This is too naïve and optimistic. Most contemporary constructivist positions, such as Giddens's (1984) structuration theory, are too balanced between agency and structure, compressing both into the mid-range 'actual' level (Jessop, 2005), where the connections between them appear too easy and available, and therefore we persistently overestimate the influence our ethics, meanings and the types of voluntary actions to which we are currently limited can exert on deep structural forces, processes and structures.

We can of course protest in the realm of symbols and act in the mid-range realist realm of situations and events, but the tentacles of structural forms that pre-exist us are everywhere and they restrict us every day, constantly preventing us from acting upon them in any meaningful, transformative way. In the deep intransitive realm all liberal politics are reduced to gesture politics. Neoliberalism's market logic restricts us as long as we remain enmeshed in it and our livelihoods remain dependent upon it. We can't wake up each morning and reinvent society, the economy and their institutions, but neither can we reduce powerful systemic forces and processes to norms, rules, conventions, speech-acts and language. Firmly established institutions have the power to influence things in the material world: think, for instance, of the probabilistic relationships between neoliberal politics, globalization, risky investment banking, rapid deindustrialization – or for that matter, rapid industrialization (see Shen and Hall, 2014) – burgeoning criminal markets, and repressive securitization and criminal justice practices. The consequences of neoliberalism's deep restructuring forces have created the divisive social conditions in which people now live.

Critical realism is also useful in that it sees *absence* as having a probabilistic causative influence on our lives. For instance, neoliberal restructuring forces do not mechanically determine harmful criminal actions, but, in the absence of welfare, which would induce further material desperation, or the absence of the politics of solidarity, which influences the way we mediate our relations to the social whole and each other, there is a high probability that criminal markets would expand and harmful crime would increase.

To understand these probabilities more clearly we must distinguish between nature and the social world. The former is amenable to deep and widespread empirical analysis whilst the latter is not. The social world is driven and shaped by real forces, but these forces can be changed by agents – as long as they are actually acting on the forces, of course, rather than simply gesturing towards them and pretending to act. Unfortunately, positivism and empiricism can detect only the symptoms, not the underlying causal/influential forces themselves, and therefore cannot guide relevant action. Whereas social constructionists and postmodernists dissolve the reality of these forces in language, discourse and subjectivity, orthodox structural Marxists gloss over the problem of subjective agency by dissolving it in crude, outdated notions of ideology as the obfuscation of truth or the hegemonic 'manufacture of consent' imposed on the individual – we will present a more sophisticated conception of ideology later when we look at *transcendental materialism*.

Most critical realists assume a relatively autonomous human agency but they insist that agents must understand ontology – what human beings and their natural and social worlds actually are – before they understand epistemology. To the critical realist, all idealist positions such as interpretivism, constructivism, discourse theory and post-structuralism are premature and one-dimensional. We can talk, but without some inkling of what sort of forces act underneath our everyday lives we have little of substance to talk about. By ignoring or glossing over underlying structural forces and generative mechanisms and their influence on the events that shape our lives, social science restricts itself to *symptomology* rather than true *aetiology* (Hall, 2012a).

For Bhaskar (1997), three ontological dimensions of social reality are open to epistemology, and by extension, are also open to agency and politics:

1 empirical: experiences of knowing subjects
2 actual: events and subjective experiences
3 real: underlying generative mechanisms that cause the events that are open to experience.

Bhaskar's (1997) 'depth realism' opens up to analysis an intransitive dimension underneath Hume's doctrine of empiricism and Kant's doctrine of subjective knowledge and ethical imperatives. This is of course unpopular with liberals and postmodernists, some of whom react with narcissistic fear and loathing at the very thought that deep structures and processes might have some influence on the way we live (see for example Turner, 2010). However, increasing our knowledge of deep structures allows us to make better judgements, or at least raise suspicions, about the validity of all the competing subjective knowledge claims and theories that emanate from various positions in today's poststructural constellation of identities and interest-groups. There is something underneath our social conversations, social relations and subjective interests, and we need to have some idea of what it is, no matter how complex, ever-changing, intellectually disturbing and politically daunting it might be. In this way, critical realism moves us beyond empirical realism (positivism and empiricism), transcendental idealism (hermeneutics, interpretivism, constructivism) and even social relations (conflict theory, Marxism, feminism) to ground knowledge in deep structures, processes and generative mechanisms.

Depth realism is not deterministic. Events observed by empiricists are not causal mechanisms but symptoms, which may or may not have some degree of 'knock-on' causality but not deep generative causality. All causes must involve social actions performed by human beings. However, despite the relentless call to 'agency' and 'empowerment' that pervades liberal social science, most social action is unconscious, routine, enforced or willingly obedient in a social world whose structures and processes are external to the subject. Therefore causality cannot be understood solely by understanding actors' meanings and the path to transformation cannot be brought into relief by simply repeating *ad nauseam* the mantra of autonomous agency, choice, indeterminacy and complexity in human meaning, desire and action. We need to go deeper and develop sophisticated conceptualizations of the contexts in which human meaning and action are generated, systematized and reproduced (see Sayer, 2000). Giddens's (1984) notion of the structure as simply institutionalized repetition of action is superficial and simplistic; today's capitalist institutions and the system in general require *controlled transformation* of meaning and action (see Boltanski and Chiapello, 2007), and we need to know why the vast majority of actors continue to appear as if they are choosing reproduction by means of controlled transformation rather than substantive transformation.

However, what Giddens has in common with Bhaskar and other critical realists such as Archer (1995) is that their transformational model of social activity operates with a duality of structure and agency. In other words, although the structure and the agent interact, they are seen as ontologically (in their nature of being) different. People act unintentionally to reproduce structures yet they possess the relatively autonomous agency required to challenge them, but their agency tends to be shaped and guided by unconscious motivations that are reproduced by the tacitly accepted knowledge they learn as they are doing things in the conditions created by the unintended consequences of their own structurally coordinated actions. Therefore critical realism's theory of social dynamics is based on the idea that acted out reasons guided by the 'natural necessity' that arises in the ontological and gridlocked logical depths of an existing social system operate as causes in that social world.

Bhaskar (1997) tried to go a stage further than Giddens, Archer and others in his understanding of how the controlled actor can become the real political actor. In his dialectical turn, Bhaskar, rather than upturn Hegel like Marx did, adds a fourth term to Hegel's tripartite framework of identity, negativity and totality: praxis (Norrie, 2010). He also changes the concept of identity to 'non-identity', which indicates the real ontological differences, real negativity and real contradictions that make up the social world, which can be changed only by agentic action informed by deep knowledge of structures and generative processes. He uses the concept of *totality* to explain how all entities and layers of being are embedded in each other. Parts may have some relative autonomy, but they are all dependent on each other and the broader relations within the whole. The totality is a therefore an interdependent *constellation*, a term first developed by the critical theorist Walter Benjamin (1999). Human agents who seek to transform the social world must be practical at the same time as being aware of their connectedness with others in totalizing systemic relations. Bhaskar agrees with Marx that only by orientating practical activities to the totality can the agent's actions become truly and simultaneously real, ethical and political. The totality is structured by what Bhaskar calls 'generalised master-slave-type relations', which are simply imbalanced power relations that have harmful consequences for those in subordinate positions.

What is absent can be expressed in positive causal terms, like a monsoon that does not occur and badly affects crops. Negativity, as we have seen in our criminological example of welfare above, is therefore also causal and absence is also transformative; it can change the nature of a thing by absenting what was in favour of the thing becoming what it was about to be before something was taken away. Since Parmenides, elite philosophers have discouraged talk of transformative absence in the social and political world, even though it happens in the real world all the time, preferring instead to focus on surrogate positive conceptions of the totality. It is possible to imagine substantial political, cultural and socioeconomic transformations caused by absence, or at least diminution. The human agent can trigger negativity and cause transformative absence or diminution by simply refusing to participate, which is the principle behind non-violent resistance such as a strike (Žižek, 2008). For alternative and more substantive examples, imagine the positive transformation of our lives after the absenting or diminution of, say, stockpiles of weapons, large corporations, the private right to create debt-generated capital, corrupt politicians, tribal identities, the entitlement to own large areas of land, or the sociosymbolic status attached to luxury consumer items and the desire to own them. On the other hand, harmful transformations can be caused by the absenting or diminution of social recognition and nurturing, democratic politics, intellectual life and education, economic participation, stable communities, welfare support and so on – but, of course, in the neoliberal era, knowing of such harmful consequences does not require much imagination.

Plato (1968), knowing that humans have a sense of transformative non-being learnt by long experience in the natural world beneath the transcendental ideal world, substituted the idea of the negative with *difference*, the idea of a *differentiated positive*, which has stayed with us in Western philosophy right up to Foucault's (1970 *passim*) hopelessly superficial classification theory. This ancient Platonic paradigm, reproduced and developed by the West's social elite to stifle ideas that might emerge in the everyday world to inspire wholesale political transformation, has trapped our thinking and action in the positivist-empirical and actual realms with little knowledge of the causative properties of negativity and absence. This has obstructed intellectual and political movement into the realm of the real to enact the transformation made possible by a wholehearted concept of negativity. It has eviscerated politics because, to cut to the chase, the *initial taking away* of power, wealth and other positive attributes and entitlements has always been at the forefront of social transformation. Without a sense of transformative non-being we are reduced to *either* the abstract universalism of Kant *or* the abstract radical particularism of Nietzsche, the existentialists and the poststructuralists (see Norrie, 2010). The ethos of radical universalism and negativity has been discouraged. We no longer think about real action, either universal or particular, with the transformation of the totality in mind. The political catastrophes of dialectical materialism in the twentieth century have discredited the whole idea because the positive power taken away from the ruling class was reclaimed by brutal self-appointed bureaucrats to once again negate the negation of the subjugated (see Žižek, 2001).

So far so good, but there is an important sense in which Bhaskar misunderstood Hegel. His claim that Hegel focused on epistemology rather than ontology is simply not true. Hegel's (1979) famous aphorism 'the spirit is a bone' tells us that he did not think that pure immaterial thought would lead us to the end of history as the Idea (Žižek, 1993; Johnston, 2008). He knew that difference is real and not simply ideal.

Because Bhaskar has a simplified view of the negative he could not deal with Hegel's well-known double negative. Adorno (1990) and Žižek (1993) dealt with it more satisfactorily by understanding Hegel's principle of the *negation of the negation*. This important concept gives us a clue as to why transformative absences tend not to be put into practice. In the capitalist system, the combination of the totality of interdependent relations and pressing systemic imperatives means that there is an *absence of politically effective absence* understood in subjective-agentic terms as the *compulsory refusal to refuse*. Instead, when situations demand it, we just do things – including crime and harm – as if there is no alternative.

The system is set up to make absence almost impossible as a political act. Put simply, in a system of gridlocked interdependencies and logical imperatives, total refusal to participate in some way would be disastrous for individuals who have no independent means of support. Welfare makes sure that people do not have to face the prospect of absolute poverty, so there is never 'nothing to lose' and always 'something to lose'. The impossibility of negation works on two levels. First, as we have seen, it is impractical. Capitalism makes all of us an offer we can't refuse if we want to keep our heads above water. Refusal would mean sacrificing the self in a biblical gesture, but this of course would have no effect in a cynical age in which personal sacrifice has been stripped of its symbolic efficiency, individualized and commercialized. Second, consumer culture is now very efficient at creating its own fantasized sense of absence and converting it into desire for consumer objects with sociosymbolic significance. Today the gratification of consumer-induced 'stupid pleasures' has on the whole become more attractive and important to the individual than the dream of participating in the negation of the system and subsequent social transformation (Hall et al., 2008; Winlow and Hall, 2013).

Bhaskar, by relying on a notion of the individual subject as a positive moral agent, also ignored the Lacanian psychodynamic principle that absence is the root of positive subjectivity because absence creates the libidinal desire – in the sense of vague but powerful yearnings – that gives the subject energy and material substance, thus implicating it in the socioeconomic system's causal chain. To the individual ensnared as a wage labourer, debt-peon and consumer in the capitalist system (see Horsley, 2015), the refusal to participate economically, pay back debts and gratify consumer desires as the first step in a transformative political process seems, as we have seen, impossible, suicidal and pointless.

The great flaw in Bhaskar's thesis is that there is too much talk about refusal with no inspiring vision of a positive political end, the positive vision that might displace the negation of the negation and give refusal a positive political purpose; the subject will never refuse to do what keeps its head above water unless it can see some alternative way of staying afloat. This absence drives the subject too close to the Lacanian Real, the dimension of our existence that is unseen, unnameable and terrifying. Neither is there a conception of the ideological negation of the negation, which, as we have seen, reproduces the system's positive forces and ensnares the agent in them. Since Plato, it has always been too easy for elite philosophers echoing the system's imperatives to persuade us that we should not 'tarry with the negative' too much (Žižek, 1993) but instead focus on positive practicalities. We have been persuaded that we should always hedonistically 'tarry with the positive', the system's positive reproductive forces, processes and objects. Most forms of criminality are manifestations of this positive utilitarian outlook, simply unruly means of committing oneself to the pursuit and achievement of the system's material, symbolic and expressive rewards without any sense of absence, sacrifice, negation, politics or social transformation.

Bhaskar's (2002) latter 'spiritual turn' can be seen as an attempt to fill up the absence of a negating subjectivity with a return to the transcendental Ideal. In simple terms, he looks for individuals to refuse to shore up the system by appealing to their internal 'better nature' – a positive source of negating the negation of the negation, or even refusing to negate the negation in the first place. To do this he has to *naturalize* subjectivity by positing a universal essence, a 'primary level' of love, autonomy and creativity beneath the alienating 'secondary level' of false beliefs created by ideology and culture. Thus he joins Archer (2000) in separating out the subject from the social system and placing it as a positive moral agent in a completely different order of being. Energy from this primary level, he hopes, can be released to transform oppressive structures. All we have to do is shed anything that is inconsistent with our natural essence. This idea draws upon Rousseau's mirror image of the legend of the Fall, the legend of Natural Grace. Because he had invested so heavily in a naturalized ethical ontology of human nature, Bhaskar had nowhere else to go but the 'human essence' notion and set us back on the road to Kantian idealism or the sort of existentialism that Sartre (1957) – in his early career one of its most well-known advocates – declared a failure because individuals cannot risk becoming so 'authentic' in environments of scarcity and systematized competition in which they are deprived of most virtuous choices.

Choice is very important, but capitalism has an effective way of dealing with it. In the process of *fetishistic disavowal* (Žižek, 2008), individuals repress into their unconscious what they know but don't want to know. We can see this in action in many social situations where individuals simply change the subject in conversations whenever some political controversy is brought up. In this way individuals *choose* what to repress into their unconscious yet simultaneously *act out* every day to reproduce existing structures and cultures. Individuals do not have to firmly and consciously believe in the system to reproduce it every day. Fetishistic disavowal is also active in liberal institutions, such as our very own social science, where, despite the recent financial crash, one is discouraged from talking about 'capitalism' in too loud a voice, especially in public (Winlow, 2012). Capitalism, we are told, like everything else, is complex, plural, indeterminate, in a constant state of becoming and so on, and must be represented as such. However, whether it is 'becoming' something worse or something better is another issue that is fetishistically disavowed by the injunction to 'think positively' and 'maintain hope' no matter how bad things get.

This powerful and easily identifiable theory of the double-negative relationship between the subject, choice and politics brings us to another type of realism, what Mark Fisher (2009) calls *capitalist realism*. This is cultural normalization of the fetishistic disavowal and subsequent repression of the very idea that the capitalist socioeconomic system and its fundamental exchange relation – to acquire a surplus in relation to what one gives – can be either replaced or significantly transformed. Every transformation in every dimension of human life is possible – except that one. In the post-war continuum of political catastrophism discussed above, most dualistic liberal thinking has avoided any meaningful intervention in anything other than the subjective 'self', which is seen as a potentially transformative moral agent existing in some mystical realm outside of the socioeconomic system. Capitalist realism, on the other hand, tells us that, even in the absence of firm belief, today's potential moral agent is entirely incorporated into the system and its reproduction, and resistant to the possibility of change: it is the reproductive vehicle of the political negation of the negation *par excellence*. This helps us to explain the types of pseudo-pacified criminality and corruption we see today, and indeed the punitive reaction. All the committed criminals and criminal justice technicians we have spoken to (see Winlow and Hall, 2006; 2009; Hall et al., 2008), whether punitive or rehabilitative, are quintessential capitalist realists.

Is there a way out of capitalist realism? *Speculative realists* argue that we must abandon all notions of detached, transcendental subjectivity in phenomenology, post-structuralism and postmodernism as well as positivism-empiricism. These positions give us only correlations between thinking and being, which alert us to secondary rather than primary qualities of the subject and the object. This creates the muddy waters in which intellectual evasion and political inaction and reproduction can be fostered.

Speculative realism is a contemporary philosophy that uses metaphysics to think through the 'noumenal' real without assuming that we can describe its totality (Ennis, 2011). It is a complex position, but realist criminological theory would benefit from drawing on its notion of *realist contingency*, which is grounded in a theory of macro-absence. Nature is not a harmonious, evolutionary whole but an uneven process punctuated by the impacts of huge disasters. Similarly, our histories and our lives are products of such disasters, which, if they had not happened, would have left us in a different condition. In the Anthropocene age, in which most of the effects on the world are caused by us rather than nature, we are the architects of many of these disasters, and, by extension, hold the power to negate these disasters and become the architects of our own fate (Žižek, 2010b). The highly criminogenic human-made disaster of rapid deindustrialization in the West, for instance, could have been avoided had firmer class politics been applied with a view to controlling and cushioning economic change and constructing a more rational, stable, sustainable and participatory economic system.

Therefore, the 'outside' or intransitive realm is no longer natural even in a qualified sense. Now that we have the power to dominate nature the effects of our own actions are of a greater magnitude than those of the power of nature. Slow evolutionary processes in criminal markets to some extent follow similar changes in legal markets (Hobbs, 1998), but the notable changes in the patterns of harm, crime and intensive securitization we now see in the twenty-first century are consequences of our Anthropocene disasters – wars, global warming, environmental pollution, financial crashes, rapid industrialization and chaotic urbanization, rapid deindustrialization and urban decay, unemployment, enforced population migration, disruption of settled communities, technological destruction of livelihoods, commercialization of culture and so on. These disasters are underpinned by the reproduction of a culture that values competitive individualism, aggression and domination. Speculative realists argue that we must view these disasters and their consequences dispassionately, and without optimism, as contingent realities in the 'cold world', and reflect on our role in their causation, and speculate freely on how things might have turned out differently, and might turn out differently should we choose to change our way of doing things. Unfortunately, however, this informed and reflective speculation is virtually outlawed in mainstream social science (see Hall, 2012b).

This *cold light of day*, as it illuminates the consequences of our actions, can reveal the disavowed context that demands an *ultra-realist* criminological approach, an investigation into the harmful consequences of our mistakes, the economic and cultural logics, drives and subjectivities that are actively involved in causing these consequences, and our failed political attempts to deal with them. Criminology, hamstrung by its dual fears of disorder and social reaction, its rigid pessimistic or optimistic views of human nature and its avowed intent to administrate whatever neoliberal history puts in front of it, constantly understates the gravity of Anthropocene disasters and their consequences. As we have seen, criminology will define problems only in terms of the competing 'hard' and 'soft' administrative solutions it is willing to consider.

However, the deficiency of speculative realism, and indeed the other forms of realism we have encountered so far, is that they have little to say about the role of subjectivity in disasters. They cannot explain why subjects don't seem to be able to learn from their mistakes, and why subjects seem willing to risk the infliction of harm on others and their environments in order to keep the current socioeconomic system the way it is and further their interests within it. In the act of separating out and absolving human beings, critical realism's dualism of agency and structure also reifies the abstract forces that we must confront with our ethics, rationality and politics. We can peer into Bhaskar's real dimension forever, but we won't find 'thing-like' abstract forces and processes that make us commit acts of harm without our active participation in their operation and reproduction. However, we do not want to swing the pendulum across to present a subjectivist argument, the tired old refrain that we must individually change ourselves and our everyday practices before we change the world. The world and our relationship to it are too complex and intertwined for this type of dualistic explanation.

Žižek (1989 *passim*) stands in far harsher judgement, but, partly because of that, provides us with a more penetrative and illuminating view of the subject's relation to the capitalist socioeconomic system. His work tells us in no uncertain terms that ignorance is never an excuse. We already know about the intransitive realm, or at least enough of us know enough about it to act politically, and we speculate every day about the problems we cause. What is absent in our liberal-postmodernist culture is a full embrace of the politically effective universal truth, Hegel's *concrete universal*, which can give our knowledge and speculation substance (Žižek, 2000a). However, despite the liberal-capitalist establishment's constant attempts to avoid it in political discourse, the concrete universal truth is known to some extent by most of us, but it is known particularly well, and felt experientially, by those who are pushed into abject positions in capitalism's social constellation. The totality cannot exist clearly in the current epistemological realm constructed by two centuries of CCLA and LPSA discursive activity, but myriad concrete universal representations of the totality exist 'down there' amongst those who experience the dire consequences of the system's disasters (see Hall, 2012b), such as the misery caused by the austerity cuts that followed the recent financial crash. Similarly, concealed knowledge of abstract processes *and* their related concrete universals permeates life 'up there' in the corridors of power in business and post-political administration. A cursory glance at J.Q. Wilson's *Thinking About Crime*, published in 1975, will reveal that at the time the US government *knew fine well* that their imminent neoliberal restructuring of the economy would cause social unrest and increased crime rates, for which they should prepare by strengthening public and private security systems.

Harmful crime, violence, intimidation, victimhood, cynicism, nihilism and destruction of communities are some of the substantive criminological elements of the *abject concrete universal*, the grim individual experiences that represent the totality of the liberal-capitalist system. The localized existence of concrete universals is important to a renewed realist criminological research project because it suggests that the sub-disciplines of victimology and ethnography should be combined in an ultra-realist mode if criminology is to become more courageous and offer intellectual and political support to those made abject. These are the individuals who suffer most profoundly the disasters of capitalism. They are the victims of the crimes of its corporations and politicians, but ultra-realism must also focus on the crimes of the cynical predatory individuals who live amongst them and take advantage of their concealed subjugation. Ultra-realist criminology's first moves are negative ones: to stop playing down the abjection of those at the bottom of the heap and the systemic and singular harms inflicted upon them, but also to stop playing down the extent to which some individuals who live alongside them reproduce and take advantage of the system's disrupted spaces (see Hall and Wilson, 2014).

As a first step towards a philosophical basis for ultra-realist criminology, we have to admit that Bhaskar's naturalistic metaphor doesn't quite work. There is no natural human essence of love and creativity to be released into the air, but there is, of course, as Adorno (2000) reminded us some time ago, a *potential* for it to be cultivated in a nurturing society. For Lacan and Žižek, the human essence is a non-essential void of conflicting drives, not some sort of naturalistic and inexhaustible Bergsonian 'life-force' (see Hall, 2012c). We can be loving and creative, but we can also be hateful and prejudiced, or apathetic, nihilistic and devoid of care. The core of the human being is far more contingent and flexible at the basic material level than any naturalistic or transcendental idealist metaphor can represent, therefore the symbolic environment is important. Roberts and Joseph (2005) argue persuasively that *the real is human*, not independent of the subject and the social world.

For Žižek, what connects the subject to the real structure is an *ideological fantasy* comprising 'sublime' consumer objects, variations of the master signifier 'commodity', which in turn constitutes the relationship between the human being and capitalism's system of relentless commodification and antagonistic social relations. Critical realism's telling mistake was to separate out subjectivity as the *naturally* ethical and creative agent. It is a profoundly fallacious assumption, in its own way as fallacious as the conservatives' and classical liberals' notion of the *naturally* wicked and hedonistic subject separated from the social and in need of firm external control. These two fallacious domain assumptions constitute the restrictive boundaries at both ends of criminological thought.

Transcendental materialism goes a step further than the other realist positions as it lays out the basis of a thorough psychosocial investigation of the so-called 'intransitive' realm. Transcendental materialism's fundamental insight is that although the forces and processes in the intransitive realm seem to act independently of our knowledge and activity, this realm is at the very deepest dynamic level a product of the historical accumulation of the systemic consequences of actions that are constantly and systematically *made unconscious*. We really know about these actions but we constantly deny or dismiss them as we perform them. In other words, we actually know quite a lot about the intransitive realm already and we have done for a long time. Each day we knowingly act to reproduce it, but we fetishistically deny our collusion and thus repress it into our unconscious.

The more official the institution in which we operate, the more actively we deny what we already know. The unconscious, the deep psychic realm of repressed symbols, is not the product of external repressive forces imposed on us from above. We create it ourselves by *choosing to repress* specific parts of what we know, which allows us to reproduce the system in which we live and our roles in it by acting out what we *don't want to know* and have therefore convinced ourselves and everyone else that we *don't know*. In other words, put very simply, each day we negate our own negating potential and choose what goes into and stays in our unconscious; put simply, we persistently *choose* our own unconscious into being. Constantly deconstructing and changing 'meaning' is of little use when every day we choose to fetishistically disavow the crucial bits of what we know anyway.

By re-appropriating Hegel and Lacan through the work of Slavoj Žižek, transcendental materialism offers a potent conception of subjectivity (see Johnston, 2008; Hall, 2012a; 2012c). It draws upon Lacan's (1974) three interconnected psychic realms of the Real, the Imaginary and the Symbolic. The Real, which consists of the unnameable irruptions of reality unknown to but experienced by the individual, is a source of stimulation, consternation and terror. The Imaginary is the realm of misidentification and self-deception, where, in an attempt to escape the Real's terror, the ego splits and misidentifies with spectral objects in the external world; as such it is the primary target of seductive external signs such as those produced and circulated by mass media, consumer culture and neoliberal post-politics. The Symbolic, or Symbolic Order, is the realm of symbols, customs and laws that allows us to understand and act in the world in ways that are coordinated with other people. A degree of symbolic efficiency, or rough agreement on what important things mean and how we should act in the world, is essential for a civilized existence. Symbolic Orders can be on one hand rigid, conservative and hierarchal, or on the other hand – if they leave gaps in which subjects can freely move – reflexive, egalitarian and progressive. It is the role of science, art and politics to create these gaps and allow forward movement.

Transcendental materialism's fundamental premise is that all humans are, paradoxically, hard-wired for plasticity, which carries a natural tendency to dysfunctionality; in other words, we are *naturally unnatural*. This allows us to create various cultures and practical ways of doing things in order to adapt to widely divergent environments, some benign and some difficult and demanding. Žižek uses the Lacanian concept of the Real as a void filled with conflicting and permanently disorientated drives and stimuli, which inflict the proto-subject with terrifying feelings of conflict, tension, indeterminacy and fear as she is unable to even begin to understand all the unnamed irruptions of the internal and external world on the neurological system. The proto-subject is desperate to escape the Real and pass through the constant misidentifications of the Imaginary to find some comprehensible, coherent and substantial meaning in the Symbolic. Transcendental materialism's crucial insight is that the orthodox notion that, in order to 'manufacture consent', dominant forces in the social order *impose* hegemonic sociocultural signals and norms on the subordinate and reluctant individual, which they subsequently internalize to become a 'subject', is completely wrong. Rather, the individual subject is anything but reluctant; it is a natural subject because it must *actively solicit* the trap of a coherent Symbolic Order to escape the terror of the Real and the susceptibility of the

Imaginary (Hall, 2012c). Only a subject trapped in the Real/Imaginary realm is entirely gullible and susceptible to the unsolicited imposition of signs and norms.

The Symbolic Order is temporarily 'renaturalized' as it elicits the subject's *emotional commitment* to its order of symbols and its underlying fundamental fantasy, but the gaps in the Symbolic Order – the stains on the Lacanian mirror – give the subject the opportunity to free itself for the purpose of reflexively revising or replacing the Symbolic Order itself. The Symbolic Order makes partial perceptions of reality possible and guides our actions within it; an efficient and truthful Symbolic Order is simply better at performing these crucial tasks. Therefore we are all active unconsciously and consciously in reproducing both the symbolic reality and underlying practical reality – in other words we *actively adopt and work with* the restraints and absences that liberal-humanists such as Bhaskar see as mysterious abstract, external forces. The Lacanian twist is that, as individuals driven by a primal fear of the void of the Real, we have no choice but to solicit the ideological trap that symbolic structures lay for us.

However, specific Symbolic Orders become ideologically entrenched in specific historical circumstances. When these circumstances undergo profound change, the entrenched Symbolic Order becomes redundant and dysfunctional – Johnston (2008) calls this descent into dysfunctionality *deaptation*. Deaptation can be counteracted by replacing a secure but oppressive and hierarchal conservative order with a reflexive and egalitarian order. This is the ideal solution, but the crucial point is that either order is better than no order at all. Deconstructing and abolishing all coherent Symbolic Orders in order to set ourselves 'free' as detached individuals, as we have been encouraged to do in the liberal-postmodern era, prevents us from overcoming our primal fear. Therefore this *intensifies rather than transcends* the emotional need for a coherent order of symbols, which, of course, today no longer exists. Its absence creates insatiable desire and insecurity, which we see appeased by consumer culture's surrogate order, or, where engagement with that fails, by the return of regressive collective forms such as fundamentalist religion and nationalism or the intensification of more contemporary forms such as the market and the security state. In everyday life our lingering primal fear manifests itself as *objectless anxiety* (see Hall, 2012a) – simply fear with no rational and consensually recognized object – in which a diversity of surrogate objects of fear and their associated means of comfort and security can be ideologically manufactured. This is how the liberal fantasy and praxis of total individual freedom always descends into oppressive forms of intervention and control.

Liberal-postmodernism, with its cult of indeterminacy, pragmatism, irony and contingency, is the ultimate historical form of *hyper-individualism*. Because there can be no true individuation without some sort of collective existence to affirm identity (see Simondon, 1964), liberal-postmodernism has set us up for permanent insecurity and, therefore, driven us to *actively solicit* forms of repressive external control. Worse still, we fetishistically disavow our active collusion in the repression we bring on ourselves and blame it on imaginary external forces, such as 'biopower', 'patriarchy' or the 'iron cage of bureaucracy'. We have allowed these imaginary substitute objects to be ideologically manufactured and presented to us by our refusal to address the real causes of our objectless anxiety, all of which are associated with the unstable, unpredictable and divisive liberal-capitalist system.

The criminological aspect of transcendental materialism's philosophical framework concerns the orientation of human energy. If Soper (1995) is right that the theory and praxis of liberalism's immaterial *transcendental subject* evaporates the physical energy needed to activate and sustain ethical and political projects, the draining off of this energy into the realm of objectless anxiety has a number of deleterious consequences. It endlessly postpones vital political interventions. It incorporates the subject into a fantasy of anticipated loss, not simply a basal feeling of lack or a melancholic memory of some loss in the past, but the constant feeling that the subject is about to lose some object of desire in the immediate future (Žižek, 2000b). This loss combines with liberalism's endless postponement of real political intervention in the capitalist system to produce the generalized feeling of an impending loss of wealth, status and security with no political means of averting it or receiving compensation. Thus a tendency to fantasize and desire a return to liberal-capitalist fundamentals pervades the air. This fantasy of an impending fall with no safety net is behind this fundamentalism, which flourished and acted as the powerful ideological advocate for the ascent of neoliberalism after 1971, when capitalism once again began to descend into recession despite the efforts of the Keynesian stabilization infrastructure.

At the core of capitalism's fundamental fantasy is a depiction of a socioeconomic rags-to-riches situation that never existed for the majority, a world full of opportunities for poor individuals to turn a buck and achieve wealth and status. Now, in the post-political era of capitalist realism, the fantasy of achieving some security and face-saving status as a lone individual in a competitive-individualist system returns as the only feasible strategy. It is this ubiquitous fantasy of impending loss and the return to fundamentalist solutions, and not simply Merton's (1938) socially-structured inequality of capacity, that places strain on the precarious individual's likelihood of remaining within the law and diffuses criminogenic tendencies throughout the social order from the ghetto to the boardroom (Dean, 2009; Passavant, 2005), which are now leading to systemic corruption (see van Duyne, 2014).

Most individuals involved in crime for selfish non-political reasons are not transgressing liberal-capitalism's Symbolic Law, or the Big Other as the unspoken set of values and customs that sustain the system's existence. Both have ceased to exist (Winlow and Hall, 2012). They are merely transgressing its prohibitive norms and technical laws, which function to prevent the subjective drives and desires the system incites from overheating and collapsing social life into violent competition. Real radical evil is compliance with the Law and the normative-legal structure for pathological reasons that are energized by the system's obscene Real – the exploitation, greed, envy and amour-propre that have been institutionalized and reproduced as sources of libidinal energy and drivers for everyday action (Žižek, 2000b; 2010b).

Interpersonal competition, which shoves in each individual's face the allure of winning and the fear of losing, is capitalism's primary device for eliciting and organizing human energy, and is therefore ubiquitous (Hall et al., 2008). In any human interaction in any nook and cranny of this competitive-individualist socioeconomic system energized by these obscene drives, everyone is automatically a potential *real threat* to anyone else's livelihood, status and identity (Hall et al., 2008). Identity-groups cluster together for protection and to benefit from the security the most successful amongst them have achieved. At the same time the culture of objectless anxiety allows specifically selected individuals and groups to be represented – sometimes appropriately but usually falsely – as a greater threat than anyone else. As the quest for symbolic efficiency is abandoned and reality melds into neoliberalism's mass-mediated fantasy, it has become increasingly difficult to tell which threats are real and which are constructed, either in the generality or in any given situation. Neither the neoliberal right's cynical naturalistic assumption that everyone is a threat nor the liberal-left's naïve idealist assumption that no-one is a threat give us any analytical purchase on the reality of our current situation; over-commitment to one or the other would leave the individual either paranoid or defenceless.

However, one has to marvel at liberal-capitalism's ability to invoke and harness such powerful, potentially destructive libidinal drives and desires without descending into violent chaos. The possibility that this descent might occur if we allow disciplinary normative systems to run down has been a motif in conservative dystopian philosophy and literature from Shakespeare and Hobbes to Golding and McCarthy. Conversely, the idea that it will probably never occur because such destructive drives and desires don't really exist has been celebrated by the liberal-left since Rousseau. However, a serious realist analysis of our current situation would compel us to acknowledge the abundant existence of numerous corrosive forms that are engendered as these drives and desires are provoked into being and harnessed to the economy. Unforgiving interpersonal competition, inequality, hostile separatism, racism, sexism, egotism, suspicion, fraud, corruption, violence, securitization and punitiveness are merely some of the crude visible symptoms that lie on the surface of the complex of underlying forces activated by the system's constant provocation of anxiety and obscene enjoyment. Yet thus far these inherently potent and disruptive forces seem to have operated throughout the industrialized West without causing too many unmanageable eruptions of unrest and violence or requiring an intolerable degree of repression and securitization. We could argue, however, that recent incidents such as the London riots of 2011 and the Ferguson riots of 2014 are two of the most spectacular amongst many other *concrete universals* which suggest that the point of intolerability is being approached in some of the most badly affected locales from which the *abject perspective* on capitalism's destructive forces is notably clear.

To explain this remarkable and rather unstable situation we must understand the basic principles of capitalism's *pseudo-pacification process*. This gives us an insight into how liberal permissiveness and conservative repression, often seen to be in opposition, actually operate together as complementary cultural forces in the dynamic psychosocial process that drives forward the capitalist economy. This process has been explicated in depth and detail elsewhere (see Hall, 2007; 2012a; 2015a), but here we present its primary elements as a simple breakdown:

- From the late fourteenth century, beginning in England and appearing later in Europe, arbitrary interpersonal violence in public space consistently declined up to the mid-1950s, and a similar phenomenon occurred over different time-scales in other capitalist nations.
- This decline in interpersonal violence occurred despite the establishment of a white, patriarchal bourgeois elite as the dominant social group in an unequal and hierarchal social order.
- During the same period there seems to have been an increase in non-violent abstract crimes throughout the social structure.
- The fundamental driver for the decline in violence was not an increase in the ethos of civilization and progress but the emergence of a dualistic economic need for pacification in an emerging market economy.
- The two primary interactive functions of this dualistic economic need for pacification are:

  1 the protection of property rights and the reduction of violent interactions between traders to *enhance safer trading activity* throughout the nascent market economy's arteries and nodes – this provided a crucial condition for expanding the *production and circulation of commodities*;
  2 the sublimation of destructive and repressive physical aggression into *functionally aggressive* yet physically pacified rule-bound competition for wealth and status represented by the acquisition and display of sociosymbolic objects in a burgeoning consumer culture – this expanded the *demand for commodities*.

- Capitalist market economies cannot become efficient and expand under conditions of *arbitrary physical violence*, but neither can they do so under conditions of *institutionalized altruism*, especially where there may be unpredictable swings between the two.
- Mediaeval Distributivist customs and laws that attempted to institutionalize altruism and a modicum of social justice in the everyday

economy – such as those restricting trading activities and prohibiting usury, price undercutting and low wages, and those limiting maximum wages and profits above the level of 'sufficient livelihood' – were repealed.

- New laws and customs were introduced to simultaneously (1) decrease violence and (2) bypass and eventually erode the relatively altruistic customs and laws that governed social and economic transactions.

- The introduction of the laws of primogeniture and entail throughout the social structure in twelfth century England atomized the traditional defensive socioeconomic units of family and community, creating a *socioeconomic tumour*, a process of cell-division that cast out anxious individuals to participate in the development of markets as they were forced to fend for themselves by seeking contractual trading or employment opportunities.

- The combination of resentment, anxiety, ambition and excitement that characterized this new individual was the wellspring of the modern Western competitive individual, and released the libidinal energy that was to be harnessed by the supply and demand sides of the emerging market economy.

- In such a fundamentally competitive culture and economy the difficult project of dispersing altruistic love outside the parent–child relationship to the external socioeconomic world became almost impossible, and we had to settle for fake benevolentism and sentimentalism, the culture of *post hoc* charity that has over the centuries masked the functional *obscene Real* at the core of our culture.

- The modern Western competitive-individualist subject's disposition towards maintaining pacified relations became overly dependent on the corresponding expansion of opportunities to obtain material and sociosymbolic rewards, which, from the Peasant's Revolt through the American and French Revolutions to the present day, 'embourgeoisfied' both pacification and rebellion.

- The normalization and constant celebration of this form of subjectivity made projects of political and social solidarity – especially those based on class struggle – very difficult to establish.

- The pseudo-pacification process was diffused, and continues to be diffused, across the world to permeate all regions that have adopted or are in the midst of adopting the capitalist market economy, liberal politics and consumer culture.

- Over the long term the balance of the typology of common crimes shifted from:

    1 real crimes of violence and acts of domination that appeared throughout the social structure alongside crimes of desperation committed by people in absolute poverty to …

    2 increasingly abstract, innovative crimes of acquisition committed to bypass legal restrictions and secure wealth and sociosymbolic status for anxious individuals whose traditional sources of livelihood, status and identity were being constantly disrupted and absented.

The fundamental socioeconomic consequence of the pseudo-pacification process is that it outlawed arbitrary physical violence for the purpose of pacifying subjects and their relations only in such a way that they could compete against each other with more intensity. This major shift in the nature of competition, caused by dampening down its potentially violent strategies and consequences, allowed *relatively safe libidinal energy* to be generated in huge abundance and supplied to the project of expanding markets and production. In transcendental materialist terms, the pseudo-pacification process was a complex dualistic form of *permanent managed deaptation*, the systematic disruption of ideologically and culturally coherent subjectivities and socioeconomic ways of life and their replacement by symbolic inefficiency, constantly dislocated subjectivities and unstable yet dynamic markets. Liberal-postmodernism's celebration of symbolic inefficiency has made a telling contribution to capitalism's final historical movement to its globally dominant neoliberal phase.

The pseudo-pacification process is maintained by the prevention of the establishment of any new symbolically efficient ideology and political arrangement that might transcend both the ancient pre-capitalist hierarchal orders and the modern disruptive capitalist marketization process to create a new, stable socioeconomic order. Liberals tend to accept capitalism because they think that any attempt to establish a new altruistic order will end up as a totalitarian nightmare and the return of some variation of the old oppressive order (see for instance Butler, 1993; Holloway, 2002; see Hall, 2015b for a critique). Thus the stable and just community, existing partially as a *memory* of unfinished projects that once operated in reality, but largely as a *fantasy* whose objects have been completed only in the imagination by centuries of nostalgia, has become the general *lost object*, the source of the fundamentalist fantasy. Absence creates desire, and the desire for love and stable community generates and reproduces immense libidinal energy that can be tapped by the corporate political, media and advertising complex that serves the circulation of today's symbol-rich commodities. Relentless yet ideologically disavowed socioeconomic disruption and competitive individualism structure reality, whilst, where the market fails to deliver enough in real terms to maintain the credibility of its fantasy, diverse *replacement fantasies* of lost collectivism – volkisch nationalist groups, fundamentalist religious sects, roots ethnic groups, neo-tribes, the cosmopolis, the 'multitude', street gangs, organized crime families and so on – structure politics and culture in the post-social milieu.

The current cultural landscape is littered with the debris of two centuries of failed revolutions and rebellions. Advanced capitalism's permanently disrupted and unstable socioeconomic order is shored up by a giant *glocal* shadow-economy of precarious part-time, temporary unofficial work and illegal markets seamlessly woven into the legal economy. This chaotic milieu is a product of neoliberalism's triumph and the working class's failure to coalesce into a *class for itself* and establish in reality its dream of collective ownership and social justice. It was misled by the liberal-left intelligentsia, whose fear of confrontation and loss created a *politics of compromise* that eventually descended into the current form of competitive intersectional identity politics we now see fully incorporated into the neoliberal system as the safe, approved opposition. Many former working-class individuals feel betrayed, melancholic, resentful and cynical in the wake of the liberal middle-class's withdrawal of their tentative support for confrontational class politics. Subsequently, they are disinclined to embrace the latter's vision of a bright cosmopolitan future of multicultural tolerance and social justice and are more likely to drift into nationalistic or criminal groups (see Winlow et al., 2015).

Whilst the mega-rich winners in neoliberalism's restructured economy ascend into an exclusive metropolitan cloud (Atkinson, 2014), the intensification of the socioeconomic competition between atomized and largely apolitical individuals creates an increasing supply of losers amongst the former working class. They are deposited in the precarious shadow-economy, a patchwork of impoverished and relatively unregulated parafunctional socioeconomic spaces (see Atkinson and Parker, 2011; Hayward, 2012b; Hall and Wilson, 2014). Whereas many of the losers sink into the depressive hedonia of late-night TV, pornography, computer games and marijuana (Fisher, 2009; Dean, 2009), and others try to avenge perceived betrayal and retrieve lost collective identity in melancholic forms of fantasized nationalism such as the White Patriot Party, Golden Dawn or the English Defence League (see Garland and Treadwell, 2012; Winlow et al., 2015), some of the more energetic individuals have bypassed the ranks of the neoliberal era's mobile entrepreneurial workers (see Sassen, 1988) to recreate themselves as illegal entrepreneurs in burgeoning criminal markets, most of which operate off governments' statistical radar.

These unregulated spaces of both the cloud and the grounded shadow-economy are conducive to the operation of *special liberty*, the sentiment that one is entitled to do whatever it takes to participate in profitable market activity and achieve economic security and social status, even if it risks the infliction of harm on others and their social and physical environments (Hall, 2012a). This indicates the social diffusion of the dark side of the bourgeois competitive-individualist mentality, constantly practised by big business and professionally hidden from view by politicians and mass media. In the absence of an alternative political vision and a project of truth and solidarity, the 'crimes of the powerful' and the mentality behind them, albeit on widely differing scales of operation between the oligarchic top and precarious bottom of the socioeconomic order, are becoming the model for the 'crimes of everyone'. The sheer scale of neoliberalism's social divisions, the intensity of its obscene drives as they fuel competitive individualism, and the precariousness of its means of livelihood, are combining to place significant strain on the pseudo-pacification process's ability to sublimate the energy of anxious individuals and orient it towards legal and socially acceptable activities in economy, culture and politics. This is the basis of the criminological reality of advanced capitalism in the twenty-first century.

7

CONCLUSION

Approaching the reality of our times

The context of this criminological reality is global capitalism in a condition of permanent intensifying crisis and insecurity. The basis of the crisis is a human-made consequential reality, and the attempts made by left-liberal intellectuals to explain all representations of the crisis as products of the *politics of fear* are becoming increasingly implausible and counter-productive. Of course some are, and carefully distinguishing between real consequences and ideological exaggerations is one of ultra-realist criminology's most important tasks. For instance, into which category do the recent BBC child-abuse revelations or reports of the new cyber-market in fake prescription drugs fall? However, underneath all this, the very real process of global resource depletion means that, even in the recently dynamic BRIC nations, the underlying growth in the real economy required to tempt investors to invest and banks to create money as debt-generated capital is entering a period of slowdown and eventual decline. The principal strategies for restoring growth from the long recession that appeared in the 1970s were the reversal of the global flows of trade and capital and the creation of abstract financial markets (Varoufakis, 2011). The explosions of personal debt and crime during the socially destructive deindustrialization process in the West and the fall of communism in the East, the resultant massive increase in securitization and imprisonment, and the austerity cuts and immiseration of the poor that followed the recent financial crash, were examples of the failure of these methods to compensate for the shortfall in real growth (Horsley, 2015). Permanent slowdown means that a large proportion of the global population will find it increasingly difficult to find meaningful and legal economic participation and livelihoods.

But hold on a minute. Despite all these problems, which should have caused huge increases in crime and social unrest, isn't crime declining internationally, isn't social unrest sporadic at best, isn't violence at an all-time historical low, and isn't liberal-capitalism the least worst of all possible systems currently leading us into a better and more sociable future? In our brief look at the *pseudo-pacification process* we have already seen how physical violence and social unrest are temporarily suspended in the dynamic realm of sublimated sociosymbolic competition, with its fragile promise of constantly increasing opportunities to achieve personal wealth and social status. Besides, although the pseudo-pacification process does seem to have reduced physical violence in the public sphere, a significant amount of residual violence, bullying and intimidation – especially the abuse of women (DeKeseredy and Dragiewicz, 2014) and children (Radford et al., 2011) – continues in hidden private spaces. The 'crime-decline' thesis is not at all watertight. It is more likely that today's empirical research in criminology, confined to the phenomenological dimension of perceptions and observable events, is focused on standard volume crimes that are sinking into obsolescence (Kotze and Temple, 2014). If we are indeed largely restricted to measuring obsolescence, it looks likely that the criminological canon – inclusive of its mainstream and quasi-radical dimensions – is entering a historical phase in which most of its data, methods, theories and underlying assumptions are also becoming obsolete.

However, we cannot simply dismiss the crime-decline argument. Some traditional crimes such as vehicle theft and burglary are certainly declining in reality quite markedly (Van Dijk et al., 2007), but whether the underlying reasons for these declines indicate any real and generalizable progress in the liberal-capitalist way of life is another question. The whole business of producing crime data and constructing an empirical basis for criminological theory is shot through with problems. We have already seen that empiricism gives us a highly restricted perspective on the world, but the general philosophical problem is exacerbated by numerous technical flaws specific and intrinsic to mainstream criminological research. Although some argue that crime surveys are of some limited use (DeKeseredy, forthcoming), others argue that they are bedevilled by methodological flaws that often seem insurmountable (Young, 2004).

Many of the crime types capable of being 'measured' by the static instrument of the crime victimization survey are certainly moving into obsolescence (Farrell et al., 2010). The big crime victimization surveys are restricted to the countries of the old industrialized West, which are historically heavy on welfare and securitization and regulated by sophisticated rhizomatic criminal justice systems. Their consumer-service economies are replete with myriad imported commodities and lurid forms of entertainment that are either cheap or free, a situation that renders many acquisitive and expressive crimes – such as burglary, theft of electronic goods, twoc'ing or voyeuristic sexual harassment – irrational and redundant, simply not worth the effort and the risk. The surveys cover only a small number of countries, and they suffer from small, inconsistent samples, low response rates and the failure to penetrate low-income high-crime locales where criminal markets are most active and 'victimless crimes' most numerous. The surveys also suffer from systematic undercounting, and they are restricted to the capture of events as experiential phenomena (Currie, 2009). At the outset they are hampered by poor conceptualization of their objects of study, which are largely restricted to legal definitions of increasingly obsolete forms of crime. Invisible and significantly harmful crimes such as domestic violence, harassment and intimidation are consistently underrepresented (Pakes, 2012).

The crime decline mirrors the crime explosion in the 1980s and early 1990s insofar as it is unequal in terms of its social and spatial differentiations (Dorling, 2004; Parker, 2008). 'Street crime' tends to be concentrated in impoverished locales, while 'suite crime' is largely hidden by the numerous methods of concealment available to wealthy and powerful organizations. The unknown dark figure of crime, combined with the localization of 'street crime', renders regional and national statistics virtually meaningless except as initial comparative indicators across time and space. Many crimes that some members of communities regard as victimless, and some indeed might regard as beneficial, yet inflict long-term harms on individuals and communities – such as tax evasion, organizing sex work, distributing smuggled cigarettes and alcohol, dealing in illegal and pre-scription drugs, distributing stolen goods and working in the shadow-economy with no health and safety regulations – obviously do not appear on victimization survey statistics (Kotze and Temple, 2014).

Any decline in specific volume crimes will make the overall figure appear to decline if it is not adequately differentiated, which of course allows political parties and indeed the liberal-capitalist system itself to use the 'crime figures' for general image-management purposes. The wild swing of the distortions between sets of causes is transparent: the liberal-right blame any apparent rise in crime rates on the moral failures of individuals and cultural groups, but when they appear to fall it is put down to good management of the economy and the restoration of the normal progress guaranteed by capitalism and liberal parliamentary democracy. When things look worse it's down to the individual, when they look better it's down to the system. The liberal-left, as official opposition, tend to reverse the formula, exonerating the individual and blaming specific repairable aspects of the system. Both the dominant and subdominant political groups in their own ways separate the subject from the system, which means that in the main, as we have seen, we are denied sophisticated analyses of the system's ideological incorporation of the subject.

Ultra-realist criminology must transcend the restrictions placed on research and theorization by the mainstream and the official opposition, without resorting to any easy and regressive move back to unrecon-structed conservatism or Marxism. Where some might claim that the statistical 'crime decline' renders a move to ultra-realism unnecessary, the unreliability of the statistics, an understanding of the intrinsic fragility and corruption of the pseudo-pacification process, and the role of repression and seduction in the reduction of crime and violence, would suggest precisely the opposite. We have already briefly examined some of the *technical flaws* in the research process. A further brief examination of some of the main *socioeconomic factors* behind the differentiated statistical crime decline can show us quite clearly that they do not give us cause for incautious optimism.

Since the 1990s there has been a demographic shift in Western populations, which now comprise more old people and fewer young people. Thus we see an obvious reduction in the guileless, easily detectable crimes in which younger people tend to be involved. The polarized social inequality of the neoliberal era has divided society into highly securitized super-rich, rich and middle classes who are therefore far less vulnerable to crime, and a badly securitized poor, reliant on cheap consumer goods, who possess little of high value for criminals to steal and who are unlikely to report what they see as victimless crimes. However, the gargantuan private–public reflexive securitisation apparatus (see Farrell et al., 2010), with its smarter policing, advanced target-hardening technology and practice, digital surveillance systems, CCTV cameras, helicopters and so on, does to some extent benefit potential victims from all classes – albeit unevenly – because there are now fewer opportunities for traditional crimes. Smarter policing has probably reduced some volume crimes in reality, but it has also artificially reduced crime statistics by changing its practices of defining, acting against, recording and reporting incidents in order to meet performance targets (Guilfoyle, 2013). The recent revelations in the UK about many police services in high-crime areas asking victims to investigate their own crimes suggest to Her Majesty's Inspectorate of Constabulary that many standard volume crimes are effectively being decriminalized (Travis, 2014). This indicates that the government is turning a blind eye towards a vast amount of everyday illegal economic activity, not simply because the police lack the resources to deal with it but because without it there would be further decline in the real economy and increased social unrest.

Beneath the superficial empirical level, in the realms of the actual and the real, we have seen profound developments in the neoliberal era. We have seen the normalization and sociocultural integration of 'hybridized' illegal and legal economic activities in a shadow-economy that operates beneath governments' statistical radar (Palidda, 2013). The precarious existence of workers is shored up by a huge and expensive infrastructure of welfare, social programmes, community projects and schemes and, in a way that echoes Huxley's dystopian classic *Brave New World*, the distribution of prescription drugs to stave off the depression, anxiety and restlessness that have been afflicting individuals across the neoliberal era (Breggin, 2012). Technology and globalization have accelerated the mutation of crime and criminal markets into innovative, hidden forms and the virtua-lization of many commodities desired for an 'entertainment' lifestyle serviced by cheap drugs has pacified much criminal activity by driving it indoors and off the street (Aldridge et al., 2010).

Criminal markets are now sophisticated and competitive, riven by class divisions created on the back of the individual's relative success and failure in markets. A successful new proto-bourgeoisie drawn from all positions on the former social order dominates a defeated precariat. Many individuals are retreating from the social and political worlds into subjectivity (Winlow and Hall, 2013). Defeatism, emasculation, depressive hedonia, lack of skills and wherewithal, nihilism and lethargy drive an escape inwards, an absorption into the mass media spectacle. The world is awash with cheap, pirated or free virtual commodities such as movies, music, pornography, computer games, social media and so on, therefore many traditional *acquisitive* and *expressive* crimes – crimes committed for material gain or crimes committed to discharge libidinal energy or display positions of social domination and status – are no longer worth the risk or the effort. In a world awash with non-criminalized harms from tax-avoidance to the grinding effects of austerity and the intimidation of individuals by criminals and bullies on sink estates, criminology's refusal to approach the concept of harm is an abdication of intellectual duty (Pitts, 2008). Harm seems to be increasingly associated with despair and the retreat into subjectivity. Alongside the rise of mental health issues, the number of suicides in the USA is now greater than the number of homicides and the number of deaths caused by auto accidents (Bonn, 2014).

How do we approach the reality of our times? Our brief synopsis of the empirical realm and what we can glimpse of the underlying real reasons for the so-called 'crime decline' tells us quite clearly that most of the factors behind it cannot be assumed to be positive or progressive. Are we therefore compelled to be dystopian? In a recent book on what he calls 'realist criminology', Roger Matthews reminds us that '[c]riminology … has a long history of pessimism, impossibilism and dystopian images of the future' (2014: 52). However, pessimism, impossibilism and dystopian daydreaming are three very different terms, which, depending on how we interpret them, can be quite contradictory. Dystopian thinking, for instance, if it is in some way connected to a realistic appraisal of reality, can negate impossibilism and shake off pessimism to spur the degree and form of social transformation required to prevent the arrival of real dystopia. Think, for instance, of our 'dystopian' but probably realistic predictions of the terrible effects of global warming in the near future. On the other hand, liberalism's peculiar teleological form of utopian thinking – the idea that no matter what we see before us we are on the road to a good future anyway, so we should just carry on as we are – can relieve the pessimism and impossibilism we feel about social transformation by dispelling it from our minds without having to make it real, which leaves our destiny hostage to fortune.

The current politics of crime data in the Western world constantly 'define down' crime and harm and understate underlying criminogenic conditions in order to maintain the mood of optimism and political pragmatism. Thus, we are to believe, the world can be transformed for the better without altering the fundamental structures, processes and norms that constitute its economic, psychosocial and cultural foundations. Criminology is limited by the dual commands 'don't look up, don't look down' (see Hall, 2012b), which means that, in order to maintain optimism and pragmatism whilst avoiding realism and the return to real politics, it systematically avoids too much critical examination of the harm inflicted on others by the powerless 'down there' and the powerful 'up there'. The 'glocal' network of criminal shadow-markets consists of global arteries of illegal trade organized largely in cyber-space and locale nodes that contain real people and markets. Let's call the global markets the *criminal cloud* and the local markets *criminal vortices*. Ultra-realist criminology should be driven by an acknowledgement of the need for rigorous investigations of the symptoms and the micro-causes in both realms, and the underlying macro-causal context they share.

There is a vast constellation of vortices that can be found in any impoverished town in poor debt-ridden developing countries, or any impoverished residential area in the deindustrialized zones, where criminal markets are so seamlessly woven into everyday life that very little activity registers on the statistical radar screen (Hall et al., 2008). The postmodern liberal-left have lived in hope of both the cloud and the vortices as the organic wellsprings of new communicative networks of people and new politics. Unfortunately both are post-political, neither immaterial illusions nor unyielding material reality but spaces structured entirely by the 'rules of the game' that capitalism lays down for everyone (Coley and Lockwood, 2011). Capitalism thrives in the shadow-worlds of the clouds and the vortices, pushing security and profit and discarding those who are in any way dysfunctional to either.

Coley and Lockwood (2011) posit the cloud as a monstrous machine of control, but this is a one-dimensional Deluezian analysis. Control simply prevents the libidinal economy, which has recently been further provoked and structured by capitalist markets and diffused throughout cyber-space, from going supernova. On the dark web a vast array of commodities are instantly available, in *reality* for those who can afford them and in an endless *procession of images* for those who can't; everything from sex and handguns to fake medicines (Hall and Antonopoulos, 2014; 2015). Rules change as they modify themselves to the expanding and proliferating libidinally-charged desires that energize the cloud and turn everything imaginable into commodities, business and profit. The cloud seeks the total conversion of all singularities into pure abstract exchange value. However, the 'rules of the game' may exist in a third space beyond reality and illusion, but, because they structure and limit human action and politics, they produce *very real consequences* on a scale that ranges from material luxury for the wealthy elite down to a harmful existence of poverty, debt, insecurity, depoliticization, enforced competitive individualism and various forays into risky and alienating criminality for the 'losers' stranded at the bottom.

In the Anthropocene age the problems we face are too big for our current liberal-democratic political and cultural systems to solve (Žižek, 2010b). Burgeoning criminal markets seamlessly woven into everyday life number amongst these problems, direct results of the marketization of labour and the struggle for status in the privatized economy and post-social world of competitive individualism and revived tribalism. Redhead's (2004) notion of *claustropolitanism* – based on Virilio's (2006) claim that humanity increasingly wishes to get off the planet and leave behind the depleting, overcrowded, gridlocked and corrupt neoliberal world of mega-cities, resource wars, clamorous markets and petty consumerized struggles for social status – contextualizes Atkinson's (2014) notion of the 'metropolitan cloud' as the first actual step, both metaphorically and in some ways literally, in this process. In the vortices, the retreat of younger generations into subjectivity and fantasy is the pallid substitute for what the rich are beginning to do in reality.

Jean Baudrillard (1993) might have been right when he said that it's all turning out like the script for a very bad science-fiction novel. Some of the hyper-idealist frameworks currently emerging in criminological theory are little more than symptoms of that reaction. In essence this reactionary radical liberalism is a symptom of the hypermodern yearning for escapism, which, paradoxically, advocates not *transformation* but new modes of *adaptive conformity* to our inherited social, politico-economic and material circumstances. Alain Badiou (2002) said something similar – at the moment, judging by the way we think and what we desire, as disembodied subjects running away from reality we all, as Redhead (2004) implies, want to be 'out of this world' (see Hallward, 2006).

One minute something is forbidden, the next permitted, the next celebrated and normalized. This constant bending of the rules is what passes for 'transformative praxis' in late capitalism. Once feeding on resistance to the *Ancien Régime*, liberal-capitalism's pursuit of freedom and enjoyment now feeds on innumerable disconnected moments of fleeting resistance to its own rules, and this incoherent resistance becomes hyper-conformity and, more importantly, motive energy. The rules adapt themselves to allow through, hopefully but never assuredly in sublimated forms, the constant exploitation, duplicity and criminality that saturate the new virtual and real criminal markets. But some forms of crime that require real harms for the consumer's enjoyment, such as child abuse and fake pharmaceutical distribution, cannot be permanently sublimated because the gratification of the drives and desires behind them at some point demand *acting out* in the physical world.

If Marx (1990) was right that in the market of exchange-value commodities are ungrounded insofar as they can establish their values only in relation to the market values of other commodities, and if Veblen (1994) was right that the conspicuous consumption of such commodities defines group status, the game of *jouissance* reaches new extremes as limits are transgressed and rules are relaxed to the extent that they might as well not exist. The pseudo-pacification process must now operate at peak efficiency to contain the explosion of libido, the modulation of affects in what John Wyndham once called the 'wild riot of pointless imaginings' (in Coley and Lockwood, 2011: 86). This is not pointless to consumer capitalism, though, as the 'wild riot' of desires is systematically and relentlessly commodified. Currently establishing themselves down there in the vortices and up there in the cloud, and largely off the statistical radar, pure, unregulated, criminogenic and zemiogenic libertarian marketplaces await our new orders.

In this simultaneously seductive and threatening climate, control and security become desires not imposed on free individuals but motivated by the subject's fear of its own libidinal excess, of just how far the individual – and, he suspects with great trepidation, everyone else too – is willing to go in the pursuit of *jouissance*, the pleasure that in its excess becomes painful and destructive. Biopolitics, the management of the system and its politically inert yet libidinally active bodies, is not the malign yet productive force of Foucault's (1998) biopower. Foucault's term is redundant. Biopower no longer exists, if it ever did; it was the fundamental and impossible control fantasy of a bygone age (Baudrillard, 2007). We now see the anxious post-disciplinary subject (see Berardi, 2009) actively seeking the comfort of the biopolitics regime. The majority actively solicit the system's symbolic order, the order of exchange value and its attendant security systems, as they sense themselves as vulnerable, isolated individuals in a competitive market. They remain inspired by capitalism's consumerist imaginary, yet scared of failing to compete and win or, if they do, having their rewards taken away from them by those who do not play strictly by the rules of the game.

In this psychosocial energy trap (see Hall et al., 2008), realism is about neither optimism nor pessimism, utopia or dystopia, impossibilism or the naïve idealism and realism which, as we have seen, are two sides of the same liberal coin. Realism is about identifying and analysing the human drives and activities behind the abstract forces that structure the capitalist system, and evaluating their consequences with as much integrity and honesty as possible. Whether the picture is inclined towards utopianism or dystopianism should not matter to a genuine critical realist. Empiricism is used by liberal-capitalism's powerful ideological forces to convince us that there are problems but nothing too difficult to manage within the political limits set by our current system of parliamentary democracy and social administration. The system's elite spokespeople are lauded and remunerated well for giving this established form of utopianism as much credibility as possible. For instance, the Harvard linguist Steven Pinker, in a best-selling pan-historical work called *The Better Angels of our Nature* (2012), blends dubious empiricist pseudo-science with teleological prophecy to stop only just short of telling us that liberal-capitalism is leading us into the Promised Land at the End of History. To manifest this dream all we have to do is carry on as normal and keep trying to be as nice as possible as we communicate with each other.

Pinker's professional liberal optimism is founded upon an aversion to universal authority, which must be opposed, we are told, by a love of individual freedom and diversity. Ever since cultural pluralism and pragmatism were established as the foundations of American liberal thought in the early twentieth century, the aversion to universalism has been a motif in liberal thought (Hall, 2012a). Existentialist criminologist Ronnie Lippens (2013: 65) avers that 'Paul's universalism, admired by 21st century critics such as Slavoj Žižek, engendered a life denying, very rigid, very divisive form of life'. Žižek's riposte to this standard liberal-postmodernist critique is well-known – such universalism actually gives *positive permission* for forms of life to flourish and negate rigid structures, whereas liberal-postmodernism *negates the negation* to leave the current divisive order intact. Of more direct interest to criminologists, however, is Dews' (2008) response. He counters this sort of quintes-sential liberal-postmodernist sentiment – born of the deep fear of order and what it might impose upon the morsels of conditional freedom we believe we have won – by asking why we have to tolerate the destructive forms of life that consistently emerge to 'affirm' and establish themselves at various points in the social order. We have to take this issue further. Why do the majority of individuals actively collude in the maintenance of a supposedly liberal system that reproduces the rigid, divisive and destructive forms of life that Dews points out, and why do they tolerate the harm it has caused and continues to cause across the generations? Perhaps this is the fundamental political question ultra-realism can begin to answer.

To do this would require nothing less than a paradigm shift, a new sociological and criminological paradigm founded not on moral con-structivism, relativism, radical indeterminacy and idealism, but on universal notions of harm and ultra-realist representations of the operational actualities and consequences of the subject's disavowed drives and desires, which activate the abstract structures, forces and processes that are the dynamic foundations of our lives in the liberal-capitalist system. Such a project would require international ultra-realist ethnographic networks to challenge and displace the statistical survey industry, and a collective theory project based on the principles provided by transcendental materialism. It would leave no stone unturned in the intellectual project of representing to the best of our ability where we are right now, historical point A, which would give us clues as to what we need to do to move to historical point B. The social technicians and reformers of the biopolitics regime who now dominate liberal intellectual life simply tell us how to make life more comfortable at point A. This is neither true philosophy nor true social science, and it maroons us in a position where all criminology is in one way or another administrative criminology.

REFERENCES

Adams, D. (1988) 'Treatment Models of Men who Batter: A Profeminist Analysis', in Yllö, K. and Bograd, M. (eds) *Feminist Perspectives on Wife Abuse*. London: Sage

Adorno, T.W. (1990[1966]) *Negative Dialectics*, trans. E.B. Ashton. London: Routledge

——(2000) *Metaphysics*. Cambridge: Polity Press

Agamben, G. (2005) *The State of Exception*, trans. K. Attell. Chicago, IL: University of Chicago Press

Agnew, R. (1992) 'Foundation for a general strain theory of crime and delinquency', *Criminology*, 30(1): 47–87

Akers, R.L. (1998) *Social Learning and Social Structure*. Boston, MA: Northeastern University Press

Aldridge, J., Medina, J. and Ralphs, R. (2010) 'Collateral Damage: Territoriality and Violence in an English City', in Goldson, B. (ed.) *Youth in Crisis?* Cullompton: Willan

Althusser, L. (1969) *For Marx*, trans. B. Brewster. London: Verso

Archer, M. (1995) *Realist Social Theory: The Morphogenetic Approach*. Cambridge: Cambridge University Press

——(2000) *Being Human*. Cambridge: Cambridge University Press

Arendt, H. (1963) *Eichmann in Jerusalem*. New York: Viking Press

Atkinson, R. (2014) 'Crime, Capital and Security in London's Alpha Territory', *British Society of Criminology Conference*, University of Liverpool, 10–12 July

Atkinson, R. and Parker, S. (2011) 'The Autotomic City: The Strategic Ejection of Unruly Urban Space', *International RC21 Conference on Urban Order, Crime and Citizenship*, Amsterdam, 7–9 July

Badiou, A. (2002) *Ethics*. London: Verso

Baudrillard, J. (1983) *In the Shadow of the Silent Majorities*. New York: Semiotext(e)

——(1993) *The Transparency of Evil*, trans. J. Benedict. London: Verso

——(2007[1977]) *Forget Foucault*. Los Angeles, CA: Semiotext(e)

Bauman, Z. (1989) *Legislators and Interpreters*. Cambridge: Polity Press

Bean, P. (1981) *Punishment*. London: Martin Robertson

Beck, U. (1992) *Risk Society*. London: Sage

Becker, E. (1975) *Escape from Evil*. New York: Free Press

Becker, H. (1963) *Outsiders*. New York: Free Press of Glencoe

Benjamin, W. (1999) *The Arcades Project*. Cambridge, MA: Bellknap Press

Berardi, F. (2009) *The Soul at Work*. Los Angeles, CA: Semiotext(e)

Bhaskar, R. (1997[1975]) *A Realist Theory of Science*. London: Verso

——(2002) *Beyond East and West*. London: Sage

Bird, A. (2007) 'Perceptions of epigenetics', *Nature*, 447: 396–98

Boltanski, L. and Chiapello, E. (2007) *The New Spirit of Capitalism*. London: Verso

Bonger, W. (1916) *Crime and Economic Conditions*. London: Little, Brown

Bonn, S. (2014) 'The reality of suicide: A growing epidemic', *Psychology Today*, 31 March. Available at http://www.psychologytoday.com/blog/wicked-deeds/201403/the-reality-suicide-growing-epidemic

Bosteels, B. (2010) 'The Leftist Hypothesis: Communism in the Age of Terror', in Douzinas, C. and S. Žižek, S. (eds) *The Idea of Communism*. London: Verso

Breggin P.R. (2012) *Psychiatric Drug Withdrawal*. New York: Springer

Buccellato, J.A. and Reid, I.D. (2014) 'Obscene remainders: Neoliberalism and the gang crisis narrative', *Journal of Theoretical and Philosophical Criminology*, 6(2): 129–44

Bushaway, R. (2003) *Managing Research*. Buckingham: Open University Press

Butler, J. (1993) *Bodies That Matter*. London: Routledge

Carlen, P. (1988) *Women, Crime and Poverty*. Milton Keynes: Open University Press

——(2012) 'Criminological Knowledge: Doing Critique; Doing Politics', in Hall, S. and Winlow, S. (eds) *New Directions in Criminological Theory*. London: Routledge

Chakrabortty, A. (2012) 'Economics has failed us: But where are the fresh voices'? *Guardian Comment is Free*, 16 April

Cloward, R.A. and Ohlin, L.E. (1960) *Delinquency and Opportunity*. New York: Free Press

Cohen, A. (1955) *Delinquent Boys: The Culture of the Gang*. New York: Free Press

Cohen, P. (1972) 'Sub-cultural Conflict and Working Class Community', *Working Papers in Cultural Studies, No.2*. Birmingham: University of Birmingham

Coleman, C. and Moynihan, J. (1996) *Understanding Crime Data*. Buckingham: Open University Press

Coley, R. and Lockwood, D. (2011) *Cloud Time*. Alresford: Zero Books

Colvin, M. (2000) *Crime and Coercion*. New York: St. Martin's Press

Connell, R. (1995) *Masculinities*. Oxford: Blackwell

Cook, J. (2014) 'Calls for genocide enter Israeli mainstream', *The Blog from Nazareth*. Available at http://www.jonathan-cook.net/blog/2014-07-21/calls-for-genocide-enter-israeli-mainstream/

Cooper, C. (2012) 'Understanding the English "riots" of 2011: "Mindless criminality" or youth "Mekin Histri" in austerity Britain?' *Youth and Policy*, 109: 6–26

Crank, J.P. and Jacoby, L.S. (2014) *Crime, Violence and Global Warming*. London: Routledge.

Currie, E. (1974) 'Beyond criminology: A review of The New Criminology by Ian Taylor, Paul Walton, and Jock Young', *Issues in Criminology*, 9(1): 133–42

——(1997) 'Market, crime and community: Toward a mid-range theory of post-industrial violence', *Theoretical Criminology*, 1(2): 147–72

——(2009) *The Roots of Danger*. Columbus, OH: Prentice Hall

——(2010) 'Plain left realism: An appreciation and thoughts for the future', *Crime, Law and Social Change: An Interdisciplinary Journal*, 54(2): 111–24

Dart, R.A. (1953) 'The predatory transition from ape to man', *International Anthropological and Linguistic Review*, 1(4): 201–17

Dean, J. (2009) *Democracy and Other Neoliberal Fantasies*. Durham, NC: Duke University Press

DeKeseredy, W.S. (2012) 'The current condition of criminological theory in North America', in Hall, S. and Winlow, S. (eds) *New Directions in Criminological Theory*. London: Routledge

DeKeseredy, W.S. (forthcoming) 'Using Crime Surveys as Tools of Critical Insight and Progressive Change', in Jacobsen, M. and Walklate, S. (eds) *Liquid Criminology*. Publisher forthcoming

DeKeseredy, W.S. and Dragiewicz, M. (2014) 'Woman abuse in Canada: Sociological reflections on the past, suggestions for the future', *Violence Against Women*, 20(2): 228–44

DeKeseredy, W.S. and Schwartz, M.D. (2013) 'Confronting progressive retreatism and minimalism: The role of a new left realist approach', *Critical Criminology*, 21(3): 273–86. DOI 10.1007/s10612-013-9192-5

Dews, P. (2008) *The Idea of Evil*. Oxford: Blackwell

Ditton, J. (1979) *Controlology: Beyond the New Criminology*. London: Macmillan

Dorling, D. (2004) 'Prime Suspect: Homicide in Britain', in Hillyard, P., Pantazis, C., Tombs, S. and Gordon, D. (eds) *Beyond Criminology*. London: Pluto

Downes, D. (1966) *The Delinquent Solution*. London: Routledge & Kegan Paul

——(1988) *Contrasts in Tolerance*. Oxford: Oxford University Press

Durkheim, E. (1961[1925]) *Moral Education*. New York: Free Press

——(1970[1897]) *Suicide*. London: Routledge & Kegan Paul

Dworkin, D. (1997) *Cultural Marxism in Postwar Britain*. Durham, NC: Duke University Press

Eisner, M. (2001) 'Modernization, self-control and lethal violence: The long-term dynamics of European homicide rates in theoretical perspective', *British Journal of Criminology*, 41(4): 618–38

Engels, F. (1987[1844]) *The Condition of the Working Class in England*. London: Penguin

Ennis, P.J. (2011) *Continental Realism*. Winchester: Zero Books

Ericson, R. (2006) *Crime in an Insecure World*. Cambridge: Polity

Farrell, G., Tilley, N., Tseloni, A. and Mailley, J. (2010) 'Explaining and sustaining the crime drop: Clarifying the role of opportunity-related theories', *Crime Prevention and Community Safety*, 12(1): 24–41

Ferrell, J. (2012) 'Outline of a Criminology of Drift', in Hall, S. and Winlow, S. *New Directions in Criminological Theory*. London: Routledge

Ferri, E. (1898) *Criminal Sociology*. New York: Appleton

Fisher, M. (2009) *Capitalist Realism*. Alresford: Zero Books

Foucault, M. (1970) *The Order of Things*. London: Tavistock

——(1998) *The History of Sexuality, Vol. 1: The Will to Knowledge*. London: Penguin

——(2006) *History of Madness*, trans. Khalfa, J. and Murphy, J. London: Routledge

——(2008) *The Birth of Biopolitics: Lectures at the Collège de France, 1978–1979*. London: Palgrave Macmillan

Fraser, N. (2013) *Fortunes of Feminism*. London: Verso

Freud, S. (1979[1930]) *Civilization and its Discontents*. London: Hogarth Press.

Freud, S. (1984[1915]) 'The Unconscious', in Richards, A. (ed.) *The Pelican Freud Library: Vol. 11. On Metapsychology: The Theory of Psychoanalysis*. Harmondsworth: Penguin.

Gadd, D. and Jefferson, T. (2007) *Psychosocial Criminology*. London: Sage

Garland, J. and Treadwell, J. (2012) 'The new politics of hate? An assessment of the appeal of the English Defence League amongst disadvantaged white working-class communities in England', *Journal of Hate Studies*, 10(1): 99–122

Giddens, A. (1984) *The Constitution of Society*. Berkeley, CA: University of California Press

Gilens, M. and Page, B.I. (2014) 'Testing theories of American politics: elites, interest groups, and average citizens', *Perspectives on Politics*, 12(3): 564–81

Goodey, J. (2005) *Victims and Victimology*. Harlow: Longman

Gottfredson, M. and Hirschi, T. (1990) *A General Theory of Crime*. Palo Alto, CA: Stanford University Press

Gouldner, A. (1973) *For Sociology*. London: Allen Lane

Gramsci, A. (1971) *Selections from the Prison Notebooks*, ed. and trans. Q. Hoare and G. Nowell-Smith. New York: International Publishers

Guilfoyle, S. (2013) *Intelligent Policing*. Devon: Triarchy Press

Habermas, J. (1984) *The Theory of Communicative Action*. Boston, MA: Beacon Press

Hagan, J. (1989) *Structural Criminology*. New Brunswick, NJ: Rutgers University Press

Hall, A. and Antonopoulos, G.A. (2014) 'The Online Trade in Fake Medicines in the United Kingdom', *National Deviancy Conference*, Teesside University, 25–26 June

——(forthcoming 2015) 'License to Pill: Illegal Entrepreneurs' Tactics in the Online Trade of Medicines', in van Duyne, P.C., Antonopoulos, G.A., Harvey, J., Maljevic, A. and von Lampe, K. (eds) *Economic and Organised Cross-Border Crime in Times of Crisis*. Nijmegen: Wolf Legal Publishers

Hall, S. (1980) *Drifting into a Law and Order Society*. London: Cobden Trust

——(2002) 'Daubing the drudges of fury: Men, violence and the piety of the hegemonic masculinity thesis', *Theoretical Criminology*, 6(1): 35–71

———(2007) 'The Emergence and Breakdown of the Pseudo-Pacification Process', in Watson, K. (ed.) *Assaulting the Past*. Newcastle upon Tyne: Cambridge Scholars Press

———(2012a) *Theorizing Crime and Deviance: A New Perspective*. London: Sage

———(2012b) 'Don't look up, don't look down: Liberal criminology's fear of the supreme and the subterranean', *Crime, Media, Culture: Special Issue: York Deviancy Conference 2011*, 8(2): 197–212

———(2012c) 'The solicitation of the trap: On transcendence and transcendental materialism in advanced consumer-capitalism', *Human Studies*, 35(3): 365–81

———(2012d) 'Consumer Culture and the Meaning of the Urban Riots in England', in Hall, S. and Winlow, S. (eds) *New Directions in Criminological Theory*. London: Routledge

———(2014) 'Social Deviance', in Sasaki, M., Zimmermann, E., Goldstone, J. and Sanderson, S.K. (eds) *Concise Encyclopaedia of Comparative Sociology*, Leiden, Netherlands: Brill

———(2015a) 'The Socioeconomic Function of Evil', in Ray, L. and Kilby, J. (eds) *Sociological Review Monograph: Violence and Society: Towards a New Sociology*. Chichester: Wiley

———(2015b) 'What is Criminology About? The study of Harm, Special Liberty and Pseudo-pacification in Late-capitalism's Libidinal Economy', in Lippens, R. and Crewe, D. (eds) *What is Criminology About?* London: Routledge

Hall, S. and McLean, C. (2009) 'A tale of two capitalisms: A preliminary comparison of homicide rates in Western European and Anglo-American market societies', *Theoretical Criminology*, 13(3): 313–39

Hall, S. and Wilson, D. (2014) 'New foundations: Pseudo-pacification and special liberty as potential cornerstones of a multi-level theory of homicide and serial murder', *European Journal of Criminology*, 11(5): 635–55

Hall, S. and Winlow, S. (2003) 'Rehabilitating leviathan: Reflections on the state, economic regulation and violence reduction', *Theoretical Criminology*, 7(2): 139–62

———(2012) 'Introduction: The Need for New Directions in Criminological Theory', in Hall, S. and Winlow, S. (eds) *New Directions in Criminological Theory*. London: Routledge

Hall, S., Winlow, S. and Ancrum, C. (2008) *Criminal Identities and Consumer Culture*. Cullompton: Willan

Hallsworth, S. (2006) *Street Crime*. Cullompton: Willan

Hallward, P. (2006) *Out of this World*. London: Verso

Hayward, K.J. (2012a) 'Pantomime justice: A cultural criminological analysis of "Life Stage Dissolution"', *Crime Media Culture*, 8(2): 197–212

———(2012b) 'Cultural Geography, Space and Crime', in Hall, S. and Winlow, S. (eds) *New Directions in Criminological Theory*. London: Routledge

Heath, J. and Potter, A. (2006) *The Rebel Sell*. London: Capstone

Hebdige, D. (1979) *Subculture: The Meaning of Style*. London: Routledge

Hegel, G.W. (1979) *Phenomenology of Spirit*, trans. A.V. Miller. Oxford: Oxford University Press

Heidensohn, F. (2012) 'The future of feminist criminology', *Crime, Media, Culture: Special Issue: York Deviancy Conference 2011*, 8(2): 123–34

Henry, S. and Milovanovic, D. (1996) *Constitutive Criminology*. London: Sage

Hillyard, P., Pantazis, C., Tombs, S. and Gordon, D. (2004) *Beyond Criminology*. London: Pluto

Hirschi, T. (1969) *Causes of Delinquency*. Berkeley, CA: University of California Press

Hobbes, T. (1996[1651]) *Leviathan*, 2nd edn., ed. R. Tuck. Cambridge: Cambridge University Press

Hobbs, D. (1998) 'Going down the glocal: The local context of organised crime', *The Howard Journal*, 37(4): 407–22

———(2013) *Lush Life*. Oxford: Oxford University Press

Holloway, J. (2002) *Change the World Without Taking Power*. London: Pluto

Honneth, A. (1996) *The Struggle for Recognition*. Cambridge: Polity Press

Horsley, M. (2013) 'Relativizing universality: Sociological reactions to Liberal Universalism', *International Journal of Criminology and Sociological Theory*, 6(4): 114–27

———(2014a) 'Censure and Motivation: Rebalancing Criminological Theory', *CrimeTalk*. Available at http://www.crimetalk.org.uk/index.php?option=com_content&view=article&id=933:censure-motivation&catid=38&Itemid=41

———(2014b) 'The "Death of Deviance" and the Stagnation of Twentieth Century Criminology', in Dellwing, M., Kotarba, J. and Pino, N. (eds) *The Death and Resurrection of Deviance: Current Research and Ideas*. Basingstoke: Palgrave Macmillan

———(2015) *The Dark Side of Prosperity*. Farnham: Ashgate

Hume, D. (1967[1740]) *A Treatise of Human Nature*. Oxford: Oxford University Press

Jacoby, R. (2007) *Picture Imperfect*. New York: Columbia University Press

Jameson, F. (2010) *Valences of the Dialectic*. London: Verso

Jefferson, T. (2002) 'Subordinating hegemonic masculinity', *Theoretical Criminology*, 6(1): 63–89

Jeffery, B. (2011) *Anti-Matter*. New York: Zero Books

Jessop, W. (2005) 'Critical Realism and the Strategic-Relational Approach', in Dean, K., Joseph, J. and Norrie, A. (eds) *New Formations Special Issue: Critical Realism Today*, 56: 40–53

Johnston, A. (2008) *Žižek's Ontology*. Evanston, IL: Northwestern University Press

Jones, D. (2008) *Understanding Criminal Behaviour*. Cullompton: Willan

Kant, I. (1998) *Groundwork of the Metaphysics of Morals*, trans. M.J. Gregor. Cambridge: Cambridge University Press

Kienscherf, M. (2012) 'Security assemblages and spaces of exception: The production of (para-) militarized spaces in the U.S. war on drugs', *Radical Criminology*, 1: 19–36

Klein, M. (1975) *The Writings of Melanie Klein, Vol. 1: Love, Guilt and Reparation and Other Works*. New York: Free Press

Kotze, J. and Temple, D. (2014) 'Analyzing the Crime Decline: News from Nowhere', *National Deviancy Conference*, Teesside University, June 25–26

Kuhn, T. (1962) *The Structure of Scientific Revolutions*. Chicago, IL: University of Chicago Press

Lacan, J. (1974) *Seminar XXII of Jacques Lacan, R.S.I.*, text established by J.-A. Miller. Paris: Editions du Seuil

Lea, J. and Young, J. (1984) *What Is To Be Done About Law and Order?* London: Penguin

Leader, D. (2012) *What is Madness?* London: Penguin

Lemert, E. (1974) 'Beyond Mead: The social reaction to deviance', *Social Problems*, 21(4): 457–68

Levi, M. (1987) *Regulating Fraud.* London: Tavistock

Lippens, R. (2012) 'Control over emergence: Images of radical sovereignty in Pollock, Rothko, and Rebeyrolle', *Human Studies*, 35(3): 351–64

——(2013) 'Can one paint criminology? Interview by James Hardie-Bick', *Journal of Theoretical and Philosophical Criminology*, 5(1): 64–73

Lombroso, C. (1876) *On Criminal Man.* Milan: Hoepli

Lyng, S. (2005) *Edgework.* London: Routledge

Marcuse, H. (1987[1955]) *Eros and Civilization*, 2nd edn. London: Routledge

Marx, K. (1990[1867]) *Capital, Vol 1.* London: Penguin

Marx, K. and Engels, F. (1972[1848]) *The Communist Manifesto.* London: Penguin

Matthews, R. (2014) *Realist Criminology.* London: Palgrave Macmillan

Matza, D. (1964) *Delinquency and Drift.* New York: Wiley

Mead, G. (1934) *Mind, Self, and Society*, ed. C.W. Morris. Chicago, IL: University of Chicago Press

Meloni, M. (2014) 'How biology became social, and what it means for social theory', *The Sociological Review*, 62(3): 593-614. DOI: 10.000/1467–954X.12151

Melossi, D. (2008) *Controlling Crime, Controlling Society.* Cambridge: Polity

Merton, K. (1938) 'Social structure and anomie', *American Sociological Review*, 3(5): 672–82

Messerschmidt, J. (1993) *Masculinities and Crime.* Lanham, MD: Rowman & Littlefield

Messner, S. and Rosenfeld, R. (1997) *Crime and the American Dream.* Belmont, CA: Wadsworth

Miles, S. (2014) 'Young people, "flawed protestors" and the commodification of resistance', *Critical Arts*, 28(1): 76–87

Moffitt, T.E. (1993) 'Adolescence-limited and life-course-persistent anti-social behaviour: A developmental taxonomy', *Psychological Review*, 100(4): 674–701

Moxon, D. (2014) 'Bonger, Willem', in Miller, J.M. (ed.) *The Encyclopedia of Theoretical Criminology.* Oxford: Wiley-Blackwell

Newburn, T. (2001) 'The commodification of policing: Security networks in the late modern city', *Urban Studies*, 38(5–6): 829–48

Newburn, T. and Stanko, E.A. (1994) 'When Men Are Victims: The Failure of Victimology', in Newburn, T. and Stanko, E.A. (eds) *Just Boys Doing Business.* London: Routledge

Norrie, A. (2010) *Dialectic and Difference.* London: Routledge

O'Malley, P. (2010) *Crime and Risk.* London: Sage

ONS (Office for National Statistics) (2014) *BCS Focus on Violent Crime and Sexual Offences* 2012/13. Available at http://tinyurl.com/nb4xga

Owen, T. (2012) 'The Biological and the Social in Criminological Theory', in Hall, S. and Winlow, S. (eds) *New Directions in Criminological Theory.* London: Routledge

Pakes, F. (2012) 'Comparative Criminology', in Clark, D.S. (ed.) *Comparative Law and Society*. Cheltenham: Edward Elgar

Palidda, S. (2013) 'Re-hybridizing the Legal and the Criminal in all Activities at the Local, National and Global Levels: A "Political Total Fact" in the 21st Century Neo-liberal Frame', in Saitta. P., Shapland, J. and Verhage, A. (eds) *Getting By or Getting Rich? The Formal, Informal and Criminal Economy in a Globalized World*. The Hague: Eleven International Publishing

Parker, K.F. (2008) *Unequal Crime Decline*. New York: New York University Press

Passavant, P. (2005). 'The strong neoliberal state: Crime, consumption, governance', *Theory and Event*, 8(3). Available at http://muse.jhu.edu/login?uri=/journals/theory_and_event/v008/8.3passavant.html

Pinker, S. (2012) *The Better Angels of our Nature*. London: Penguin

Pitts, J. (2008) *Reluctant Gangsters*. Cullompton: Willan

Plato (1968) *The Republic*. New York: Basic Books

Radford, L., Corral, S., Bradley, C., Fisher, H., Bassett, C., Howat, N. with Collishaw, S. (2011) *Child Abuse and Neglect in the UK Today*. London: NSPCC. Available online at www.nspcc.org.uk/childstudy

Rafter, N.H. (2009) *The Origins of Criminology*. London: Cavendish

Ray, L. (2011) *Violence and Society*. London: Sage

Redhead, S. (2004) *Paul Virilio*. Edinburgh: Edinburgh University Press

——(2014) 'The Last of the Working-Class Subcultures to Die? Real Tales of Football Hooligans in the Global Media Age', in Hopkins, M. and Treadwell, J. (eds) *Football Hooligans*. Basingstoke: Palgrave Macmillan

Reiner, R. (2007) *Law and Order: An Honest Citizen's Guide to Crime and Control*. Cambridge: Polity

——(2012) 'Political Economy and Criminology: The Return of the Repressed', in Hall, S. and Winlow, S. (eds) *New Directions in Criminological Theory*. London: Routledge

Roberts, J.M. and Joseph, J. (2005) 'Derrida, Foucault and Žižek: Being realistic about social theory', *New Formations*, 56(1): 109–20

Sartre, J. (1957) *Being and Nothingness*. London: Methuen

Sassen, S. (1988) *The Mobility of Labor and Capital*. Cambridge: Cambridge University Press

Sayer, A. (2000) *Realism in Social Science*. London: Sage

Sedgwick, P. (1982) *Psycho Politics*. London: Pluto

Shantz, J. (2012) 'Radical criminology: A manifesto', *Radical Criminology*, 1: 7–19

Shen, A. and Hall, S. (2014) 'The same the whole world over? A review essay on youthful offending from the 1980s and youth justice in contemporary China', in *International Journal of Law, Crime and Justice*, xx: 1–19

Simon, J. (2007) *Governing through Crime*. Oxford: Oxford University Press

Simondon, G. (1964) *L'Individu et sa genèse physico-biologique*. Paris: PUF

Skinner, B.F. (1971) *Beyond Freedom and Dignity*. New York: Knopf

Smith, O. (2014) *Contemporary Adulthood and the Night Time Leisure Economy*. London: Palgrave

Soothill, K., Francis, B., Ackerley, E. and Humphreys, L. (2008) 'Changing patterns of offending behaviour among young adults', *British Journal of Criminology*, 48(1): 75–95

Soper, K. (1995) *What Is Nature?* Oxford: Blackwell

Sutherland, E. (1947) *Principles of Criminology*, 4th edn. Philadelphia, PA: J.B. Lippincott

Sykes, G. and Matza, D. (1957) 'Techniques of neutralization: A theory of delinquency', in *American Sociological Review*, 22(6): 664–70

Tawney, R.H. (1964[1931]) *Equality*. London: Unwin

Taylor, B. (2014) *The Last Asylum*. London: Hamish Hamilton

Taylor, I. (1982) *Law and Order*. London: Macmillan

——(1999) *Crime in Context*. Cambridge: Polity

Taylor, I., Walton, P. and Young, J. (1973) *The New Criminology*. London: Routledge

——(1975) *Critical Criminology*. London: Routledge & Kegan Paul

Thompson, B. and Williams, A. (2013) *The Myth of Moral Panics*. London: Routledge

Thompson, E.P. (1971) 'The moral economy of the English crowd in the eighteenth century', *Past and Present*, 50(1): 76–136

Tittle, C.R. (1995) *Control Balance*. Boulder, CO: Westview

Tombs, S. and Whyte, D. (eds) (2003) *Unmasking the Crimes of the Powerful*. New York: Peter Lang

Travis, A. (2014) 'Police telling victims to solve crimes by themselves', *The Guardian*, 4 September. Available at http://www.guardian.com/uk-news/2014/sep/04/police-telling-victims-solve-crimes-themselves

Turner, C. (2010) *Investigating Social Theory*. London: Sage

Van Dijk, J., van Kesteren, J. and Smit, P. (2007) *Criminal Victimisation in International Perspective: Key Findings from the 2004–2005 ICVS and EU ICS*. The Hague: Ministry of Justice/WODC

van Duyne, P.C. (2014) 'Greed: The Deadly Sin as Red Thread – An Introduction', in van Duyne, P.C., Harvey, J., Antonopoulos, G.A., von Lampe, K., Maljević, A. and Markovska, A. (eds) *Corruption, Greed and Crime Money*. Nijmegen: Wolf Legal Publishers

Varoufakis, Y. (2011) *The Global Minotaur*. London: Zed

Veblen, T. (1994[1899]) *The Theory of the Leisure Class*. London: Penguin

Virilio, P. (2006[1977]) *Speed and Politics*. Cambridge, MA: MIT Press

Walsh, A. (2009) *Biology and Criminology*. London: Routledge

Walsh, A. and Beaver, K. (eds) (2009) *Biosocial Criminology*. Aldershot: Ashgate

Whitehead, P. and Crawshaw, P. (eds) (2013) *Organising Neoliberalism*. London: Anthem

Wiggershaus, R. (2010) *The Frankfurt School*. Cambridge: Polity

Wilkins, L.T. (2001[1964]) *Social Deviance*. London: Routledge

Williams, R. (1971) *Culture and Society, 1780–1950*. Harmondsworth: Penguin

Wilson, J.Q. (1975) *Thinking About Crime*. New York: Basic Books

Winlow, S. (2012) 'Is it OK to Talk about Capitalism Again? Or, Why Criminology Must take a Leap of Faith', in Winlow, S. and Atkinson, R. (eds) *New Directions in Crime and Deviancy*. London: Routledge

——(2015) 'Trauma, Guilt and Shame: Some Theoretical Notes on Violent Subjectivity', in Ray, L. and Kilby, J. (eds) *Sociological Review Monograph: Violence and Society: Towards a New Sociology.* Chichester: Wiley

Winlow, S. and Hall, S. (2006) *Violent Night: Urban Leisure and Contemporary Culture.* Oxford: Berg

——(2009) 'Retaliate First: Memory, humiliation and male violence', *Crime, Media, Culture,* 5(3): 285–304

——(2012) 'What is an ethics committee? Academic governance in an era of belief and incredulity', *British Journal of Criminology,* 52(2): 400–16

——(2013) *Rethinking Social Exclusion: The End of the Social?* London: Sage

Winlow, S., Hall, S., Treadwell, J. and Briggs, D. (2015) *Riots and Political Protest.* London: Routledge

Yar, M. (2012) 'Critical Criminology, Critical Theory and Social Harm', in Hall, S. and Winlow, S. (eds) *New Directions in Criminological Theory.* London: Routledge

Young, J. (1975) 'Working Class Criminology', in Taylor, I., Walton, P. and Young, J. *Critical Criminology.* London: Routledge & Kegan Paul

——(1999) *The Exclusive Society.* London: Sage

——(2004) 'Voodoo Criminology and the Numbers Game', in Ferrell, J., Hayward, K., Morrison, W. and Presdee, M. (eds) *Cultural Criminology Unleashed.* London: The Glasshouse Press

Zaino, J. (2013) 'Attacks on US federal funding of the social sciences date back to the 1940s and will continue to intensify', London School of Economics blog. Available at http://blogs.lse.ac.uk/impactofsocialsciences/2013/06/24/nsf-restrictions-political-science/

Žižek, S. (1989) *The Sublime Object of Ideology.* London: Verso

——(1993) *Tarrying with the Negative.* Durham, NC: Duke University Press

——(2000a) *The Ticklish Subject.* London: Verso

——(2000b) 'Melancholy and the Act', *Critical Inquiry,* 26(4): 657–81

——(2001) *Did Somebody Say Totalitarianism?* London: Verso

——(2005) *Iraq: The Borrowed Kettle.* London: Verso

——(2006) *The Parallax View.* Cambridge, MA: MIT Press

——(2008) *Violence.* London: Profile Books

——(2010a) 'How to Begin from the Beginning', in Douzinas, C. and Žižek, S. (eds) *The Idea of Communism.* London: Verso

——(2010b) *Living in the End Times.* London: Verso

INDEX